Contents

INDEX ON CENSORSHIP

VOLUME 42 NUMBER 03

Culture

Supported using public funding by

**ARTS COUNCIL
ENGLAND**

Cover image: Wail Gzoly

Freedom to speak and be heard

by **Rachael Jolley**

INDEX EDITORIAL

42(3): 3/5 | DOI: 10.1177/0306422013504516

THE DEVELOPMENT OF this issue began with a simple idea that has profound consequences: it would include a special global report on the voices of those who are rarely heard. There are countless reasons why those people, and they number in their millions, are ignored, suppressed or actively censored. It may be that their mother tongue is not a mainstream language, or that they belong to a group their government fears, distrusts or simply disregards.

But this theme of ours became, too, a tale of those who do have highly audible voices – journalists, both those whose news reporting works in uncovering hidden voices and untold stories, sometimes against great odds, and those whose don't. These two strands – hidden voices and the power of journalism to make those voices audible – weave through many of the reports in this autumn issue of Index on Censorship. These two themes lie also, of course, at the core of Index's work down decades to expose the untold story and to encourage the highest standards of investigative journalism.

Journalism fails when it reports only the stories people want to be told; it also fails when it doesn't tell the difficult, uncomfortable stories that influential powers – governments, corporations, litigious celebrities – would rather were silenced. Some of the world's media edge away from the news that takes weeks to find and research. Globally, news organisations are struggling to solve the equation of what good journalism costs and how much income can be expected back from it, as well as asking whether they should produce what many would call investigative journalism, or what others would call the news. Real news costs money; it's difficult; facts have to be checked, sources talked to. Often the costs of lawyers form part of the equation, adding to the journalism balance sheet.

What we know is that the stories that are told about a country by its own citizens and by others are important – important for the country's development and important for the citizens and their sense of participation in that society. We also know there will always be authoritarian figures who want everything their own way; they want the narrative about their country to be the one that they decree; and they want anyone who criticises that story to be silenced. Technology can help get some of those stories out, and the new floating modems that are soon to be in the skies above Africa should help offer access to the web for thousands of people who currently have no way to use it. But technology alone doesn't do the job; people are the other part of the discussion.

In this issue, we tell stories of those who are fighting to continue the positive traditions of reporting. Two traditional journalists, Nic Dawes and Shu Choudhary – one a newspaper editor, the other an ex-BBC producer – are doing inspiring things to improve news reporting. Dawes, who has just left South Africa's Mail & Guardian for the Hindustan Times, helped create an investigative journalism training centre for →

→ reporters from across Africa. Meanwhile, Choudhary is one of the founders of a citizen journalism-based news operation for a central Indian community who are often ignored by the mainstream press. This is a community whose mother tongue is not widely spoken and does not have a high level of literacy. Using a mix of mobile phones and the web, Choudhary has created a news community that is ringing in its own stories that otherwise would have never been heard, and listening to those of its neighbours; his news operation is making a difference, too, not just because it is healthier if this community believes other people care about its problems. Corruption and health scandals have been uncovered and addressed. This is news that changes society.

Elsewhere in this issue are other voices that too often go unheard. Our reports from Brazil, Egypt, Mali, Azerbaijan, China, Russia and South Africa, among others, speak with people who have experienced violence, poverty and limited opportunities because of who they are, where they come from or where they live. Meanwhile, in Colombia and Honduras, journalists are fighting to get the news out, and putting their own lives in danger.

Nobel Prize winning economist Amartya Sen writes in this issue about the responsibilities for journalists in developing societies to use their work to create a better, healthier nation. It might sound like an idealistic vision (and there's nothing wrong with that) but at the heart of journalism there is a core principle about righting some wrong; making a story public because someone doesn't want it to be so; changing something for the better. Sen's influential ideas about development and freedom, and his article for this issue, have been at the heart of our special report. This influential academic has argued that we must value freedom to participate in the public and political debate as an essen-

tial part of development. Those with a lack of freedom to participate may live in an authoritarian state where only a few authorised voices are heard; or they may live in a democratic state where a particular minority group is ignored or excluded.

Citizen journalism has more of a chance to bring stories on to the public airwaves than it did in decades past. Mobile phones and the web are enormous assets. But there are still obstacles to using technology: having the money, having the signal, having the equipment, as well as having a government that might deny you the right to use those things. Access matters – so does news and the right to tell it. ▨

Sarah Brown will be the keynote speaker at the launch of this issue of Index on Censorship on 15 October in London. Sarah Brown is the co-founder of the A World at School initiative, which helped to convene Malala Day at the United Nations in July this year. She also set up PiggyBankKids, a UK charity started in 2002 to make a difference to the lives of some of the UK's most vulnerable babies, children and young people. If you would like to join us for the launch, or would like to be invited to other launches, please email David Heinemann, davidh@ indexoncensorship.org

©Rachael Jolley
www.indexoncensorship.org

LEFT: Not heard?

Rachael Jolley is editor of Index on Censorship

SPECIAL REPORT

In this section

ABOVE: A worker reads a newspaper in Kolkata

Press freedom: what is it good for?

42(3): 8/14 | DOI: 10.1177/0306422013503105

India and its media must make better use of its democratic freedoms. Surprisingly, says Nobel Prize winner **Amartya Sen,** it might be able to learn something from China

IS FREE SPEECH in conflict with the demands of economic and social development, or are they complementary? That question can be addressed at different levels of generality. It is important to understand the wide reach and pervasive relevance of

Press freedom can be most effective only when that freedom is utilised by the media fully, rather than in a biased or slanted way

this question, even when the immediate context of the discussion is a very specific comparison. The immediate reference point of this article is the comparison of China and India.

A strong belief – often implicit – in the importance of good technocratic planning for successful development (no nonsense about disorderly public discussion) used to be quite dominant in economic thinking for a long time, and it received rather little challenge until late in the 20th century. Rather than encouraging public debates, the process of governmental policy-making tended, for a long time, to rely on the presumed soundness of decisions taken by "those who know best".

That view has, however, been challenged over the last few decades, and it has been argued that press freedom is crucially important for development. Why so? The literature on the subject has highlighted, in one way or another, at least four distinct reasons in favour of encouraging and facilitating uncensored public discussion. The first reason is the intrinsic value of freedom of speech and public communication in the freedom of human beings. If it is accepted that people's freedom to do what they have reason to value is really important, then freedom cannot but be one of the central objects of development. And given that basic recognition, it is easy to see that freedom of speech and communication must be among the constitutive ingredients of development – an important component of developmental ends.

Second, seen as an instrument, the role of a free press in disseminating knowledge and facilitating critical scrutiny is a necessary requirement of informed politics, and cannot but be important for the formulation of development policies, for the enrichment of public debates on the diagnoses of the problems to be addressed, and on the assessment of policies.

Third, the protective role of press freedom in giving voice to the neglected and the disadvantaged, and thus helping the cause of greater human security, is by now well accepted. The observation that famines do not occur in functioning democracies with freedom of the press is one testament to this protective role.

Fourth, the functioning of a free press and its contribution to open public discussion are important in generating new ideas, including the formation and scrutiny of values. Press freedom also contributes greatly to the emergence of shared public standards, which are central to discussions on social justice.

Achievements of China and India

I should admit that I have been a follower of this relatively new line of thinking about development, and have argued for the importance of press freedom, and more generally for the benefits of a functioning democracy. But that immediately raises a problem, in particular when comparing China with India. I have to argue, at the risk of sounding hopelessly self-indulgent, that the possible tension – even an apparent contradiction – in my thinking may apply to others as well, since none of my beliefs on the two subjects are particularly unique.

India has had a far less restricted press than China, and has been much more of a practising democracy. And yet in terms of the standard criteria of economic and social development, China has clearly done significantly better than India. China not only has had a faster rate of economic growth (even though India's has been fast too) but, more significantly, it has achieved a higher life expectancy, fuller literacy, and a wider coverage of guaranteed health care than India (and here – unlike in the case of the rate of economic growth – India's performance is very deficient). The question that immediately arises is whether this indicates that press freedom is not really that important, and whether it may even work to the detriment of development.

I would argue that the answer to what appears to be a dilemma lies in the recognition that press freedom can be most effective only when that freedom is utilised by the media fully, rather than in a biased or slanted way. Freedom is a permissive condition, and permission is not enough to make a success of the use of the opportunity available.

The achievements of a democratic system depend on what issues are brought into political engagement. Some issues are extremely easy to politicise, such as the calamity of a famine (which tends to stop abruptly with the institution of a functioning democratic political system, as has happened in several countries, including India), whereas other issues – less spectacular and less immediate – provide a much harder challenge. Using democratic means to remedy non-extreme undernourishment, or persistent gender and caste inequalities, or the absence of regular medical care for all, is much more difficult, and success or failure here depends significantly on the range and vigour of democratic practice. There has, however, been considerable progress in dealing with some of these issues, such as particular features of gender inequality, through relatively improved practice of democracy in recent years. But there is still a long way to go to take on all the social disadvantages and injustices from which many Indians persistently suffer.

Efficiency and fragility of authoritarianism

In contrast, in China the process of decision-making depends largely on decisions at the top, taken by political leaders, with relatively little scope for democratic pressure from below. The spectacular fact that the Chinese leaders, despite their scepticism of the values of democracy and liberty, have been strongly committed to eliminating hunger and illiteracy has certainly helped China's economic and social advancement. That deserves huge applause.

→

ABOVE: Chinese Premier Li Keqiang speaks with Sonia Gandhi during a meeting in May this year

→   And yet there is an inescapable fragility in any authoritarian system, since there is little remedy when the government leaders change their priority in a counterproductive direction. The reality of that danger

India has to make much greater use of the freedom of the media, and more generally of its democratic system, than it has done in the past

revealed itself in catastrophic form in the Chinese famine of 1959–62, which killed at least 30 million people, when the regime failed to understand what was going on and there was no public pressure against its policies, as would have arisen in a functioning democracy. The policy mistakes continued throughout these three years of devastating famine. There was not only no politically significant opposition (and no criticism of the disastrous policies pursued by the

government) but the information blackout was so complete with censorship and control of the state media that government itself came to be deceived by its own propaganda and believed that the country had 100 million more metric tons of rice than it actually had. Eventually, Chairman Mao himself made a famous speech, in 1962, lamenting the "lack of democracy" because it led to mistakes in centralised planning thanks to informational deficiency.

The fragility was seen again with the economic reforms of 1979, when China took the intelligent decision of removing its huge antipathy to the market economy, and this greatly improved the efficiency of Chinese agriculture and industry. But wholesale marketisation also involved a huge retreat from the principle of universal health care coverage for all. As the axe fell on the "rural cooperative medical system", the proportion of the rural population universally covered by free or heavily subsidised health care crashed to 10 per cent or so within a few years.

Such fragilities are hard to eliminate in an authoritarian system where supportive and protective policies can suddenly change, depending on power politics at the top. An established right to health care could not have been so easily – and so swiftly – withdrawn in a functioning democracy. The withdrawal of universal entitlement to health care sharply reduced the progress of longevity in China, and China's large lead over India in life expectancy dwindled over the following two decades – falling from a 14-year lead to one of just seven years. However, the Chinese authorities did eventually come to recognise the value of what had been lost, and reversed their direction of thinking again – this time with very positive results. The reintroduction of social health insurance on a large scale (under new arrangements, including the "new cooperative medical scheme") from around 2004 helped China to have a much higher proportion of people with guaranteed health care (more than 90 per cent) than does India. The gap in life expectancy in China's favour has been rising again, and is now about 10 years. The reach of health coverage is clearly central to this trend.

To make use of press freedom and democracy

Given India's multiparty democratic practice, it has to cultivate democratic engagement in demanding universal health care and addressing long-standing neglects. This means putting pressure on the government in office but also making these priorities a part of the political demands of the opposition, since governments, especially coalition governments such as the present one in New Delhi, have to respond to the priorities set by political pressures and public demands, which can take widely diverse forms and which all compete for governmental attention and resources. Cultivating democratic engagement can be a harder task than convincing a handful of political leaders of the need for a policy change. On the other hand, if a norm of this kind is democratically established, it is less subject to the fragility to which all authoritarian

decisions remain vulnerable. In order to match China in health coverage and surpass it in resilience, India has to make much greater use of the freedom of the media, and more generally of its democratic system, than it has done in the past. The same can be said for the priority of basic education for all.

That this can be done has already been shown in India, in the use of democratic freedoms in particular states, through prioritizing public services, also allowing the pursuit of inclusive economic growth. Kerala, Tamil Nadu and Himachal Pradesh have combined the pursuit of social welfare with the cultivation of fast economic growth. Indeed, the fact that an educated and healthy labour force has not only enjoyed enhanced living standards but that it has also helped these states to quickly

In terms of the standard criteria of economic and social development, China has clearly done significantly better than India

ascend the ladder of per-capita incomes, thanks to rapid economic growth, illustrates this point with much clarity. Even at the national level there have been many successes, for example in addressing the AIDS epidemic (it had been predicted that India would be the country most severely affected by this global epidemic, but that outcome was prevented by swift public policies responses with wide reach). There has also been impressively fast legal reform to help provide more security and safety for women, which followed the public agitations after a terrible case of gang rape in mid-December 2012. The legal amendments were not as strong as some wanted, but much stronger than the previous system of laxity and inefficiency, and the →

→ amendments were enacted by the Indian Parliament within three months of the agitations.

To conclude, press freedom and democratic guarantees are necessary for making a high-performing development path secure and stable, rather than fragile, even if such reforms can be more quickly ushered in in the absence of democratic freedoms. An authoritarian country could go the way of North Korea or of South Korea, or experience varying performance of the kind China has historically had, depending on factors other than democratic social choice. There are many things of great importance that India, including its media, can learn from China, but to make use of these lessons India needs to make more, rather than less, use of its democratic freedoms and uncensored media.

As one of the principal architects of India's democratic constitution, B R Ambedkar, said with deep insight: in order to make a success of its democracy, India needs to continue and vastly expand its efforts to "educate, agitate and organise". That call to action remains substantially unfulfilled. A free press has to be more than its own reward.

©Amartya Sen
www.indexoncensorship.org

Amartya Sen is Thomas W. Lamont University Professor at Harvard University and was previously Master of Trinity College, Cambridge. This article draws on his books Development as Freedom (1999) and, jointly with Jean Dreze, An Uncertain Glory: India and Its Contradictions (2013). He was awarded the Nobel Prize in Economics in 1998

Talk back

Index invited Ferial Haffajee, editor of South African newspaper City Press, to respond from a journalist's point of view to Amartya Sen's points on press freedom.

At two titles I've edited, we have faced gags or attempted gags more than 10 times in 10 years. This pre-publication censorship (through attempted court interdict) is the most severe form. It has been attempted by multi-national corporations, a corrupt but popular youth leader, our version of the FBI, companies linked to the governing African National Congress and others of the motley crew who do not know the South African constitution.

Our constitution explicitly protects free speech and thus a free media. It has saved my bacon many times and held the censors at bay when gags have failed in court. I have often been surprised by the people we've found ourselves sitting opposite in court. There have been good democrats among them and people who helped draft the Constitution and birthed the new democracy of Nelson Mandela.

Is it as simple as them not having read the ground law or forgotten it? Not at all. It is that media freedom is great in philosophy when you are in revolutionary trenches, but very hard to stay true to when you are in power. Because power, I've seen in the past 19 years, does corrupt as money and influence are as seductive here as they are anywhere. Mandela's generation of political leaders, who lived for a larger goal and were "servant leaders" before the term was even coined, have been replaced by a generation driven instead by self-interest.

Corruption is a growing cancer. To illustrate: President Jacob Zuma has made R250 million (US$24.5 million) worth of renovations on his private estate drawing on the public purse, when the rule-books allow only R100,000 (US$9,790) for security enhancements. Relationships between the presidency and titles like City Press are brittle because public interest has clashed loudly with self-interest on this and other instances.

In addition to the gags, the South African media and its allied freedom of expression organisations have had to fight off efforts at greater state regulation and less transparency as the pace of investigative journalism has been cranked up.

Journalism in a new democracy, in which I feel myself personally invested, is a constant balance between being a critic and a patriot (the US PATRIOT Act notwithstanding, I am patriotic). We walk a tightrope between being a watchdog and recognising the role of the media to help shape society by being useful and constructive. What does this mean? It means ensuring that our coverage of health, of education and of the often arcane processes of development (bringing water, toilets, housing and broadband access to a majority of people and, in South Africa's case, dealing with a cruel AIDS pandemic) is as sexy and as omnipresent as the coverage of celebrities, powerful people and corruption.

This is not always easy as a nation turns its attention to play, sex and scandal after so many years of struggle. The country would rather not be distracted by "development journalism", choosing instead to pay attention to the seduction of the Kardashians or the next hot reality show. But covering development is a core part of our responsibility, as is ensuring that we give adequate exposure to the things government gets right.

In our case, this includes reporting on the extension of a substantial social safety net to a majority of South Africans (no other African country has such a comforting net), electricity connections, housing, and the government managing the economy fairly well through two recessions. In my case (and I can't speak for colleagues), it is also ensuring that I always refer to South Africa as "our country" and not "this country", for I am not alien to the place I was born in and where I now practise and enjoy a healthy media freedom.

With its constitutional umbrella, South Africa has developed a feisty and free media that is invested in the country's success. We are not perfect, but we are a decent fourth estate that enjoys good levels of trust from our different reading publics.

||||||||||||||||||||||||||||||||||||||||||||||||||||||||||||||||||||||||||||||||||||||||||||||||||||||||||||||||||||

In this, we have learnt well from Amartya Sen's seminal philosophy of development as freedom. As a child who grew up under apartheid and then a woman who benefited enormously from the freedom years and the ANC's policies, my journalism is not particularly geared toward the "Gotcha" mode of investigative work. It is not focused on up-ending governments or claiming scalps, though it is good when bad leaders are called to account.

My working thesis is that corruption and poor government practice and policy impact on the extension of freedom. They sap the dream of freedom and make a beloved country less than it can be. So, every time we take on a large investigation, we try to show what has been squandered or stolen in houses we could have built and identify entrepreneurs we could have encouraged and children who could have been given a better education.

Media freedom and the possibilities of democracy, I've learnt in South Africa's free years, are totally indivisible.

Ferial Haffajee is editor of the Sunday newspaper City Press in South Africa

The revolution realists?

42(3): 16/24 | DOI: 10.1177/0306422013502445

After this summer's overthrow of President Morsi, protests in the streets and political turmoil, can there ever be a revolution in attitudes to women in Egypt? **Melody Patry** and **Rasha Mohamed** report. Photos by **Wail Gzoly**

"I WAS HOPING THAT the revolution would finally rid Egyptian women of the patriarchal structure and values that have been deeply rooted and embedded in society; that they would receive the recognition they deserve, and be able to occupy wider spaces in the public sphere, especially given that they were one of the main pillars of the revolution", said Amal Elmohandes,

> ## As a young woman involved in politics, it is very difficult to have your voice heard because you are marginalised as a woman and you are marginalised as a young person

director of the women's rights defenders programme at Nazra for Feminist Studies, a research organisation based in Cairo.

The role of women in the struggles of the past two years has been highlighted in newspapers and on television bulletins. And for many there was a sense that for women in Egypt, this was going to be a time of change. "There has been a rupture between before, when access to politics was difficult for everyone, and after the revolution," said Dina Wahba, Egyptian feminist and political activist. "The atmosphere changed and people somehow romanticised the revolution."

During live streaming from Tahrir Square during the 25 January 2011 revolution, the voices of women could be heard reverberating across the crowds. Defiant and outspoken, these women and girls from all sectors and areas of Egyptian society were at the heart of the struggle leading up to the fall of Hosni Mubarak and have been emphatic in their demands for a better future. However, as the transition progressed, women's presence in public and political spheres did not reflect their role in the protests.

Elmohandes was among many women who were hopeful that life for Egyptian women was going to change after the January 2011 revolution. But the exclusion of women from top political positions, attacks on female demonstrators, and daily sexual harassment didn't stop, and some argue they have become worse.

As the streets of Cairo filled up again on 30 June 2013, leading to the ousting of President Mohamed Morsi, women participated in demonstrations on a massive scale again. With a disputed interim government in place, ongoing protests and army tanks deployed on the streets to maintain national peace, the situation remains unstable and unpredictable. Uncertainty lingers over the place of Egyptian women in this new phase of the country's development.

A powerful image that appeared on one of Cairo's walls during the revolution represents the ancient Egyptian queen Nefertiti with a tear gas mask. The mural, by graffiti artist el Zeft, is a tribute to women's bravery in battle and implicitly defends their right to equality. It is also a reminder of ancient Egypt, when women could be pharaohs and enjoyed equal status with men. Unlike in most other ancient societies, Egyptian women of the time enjoyed the same legal and economic rights as men.

Today's modernisers can draw on the strength of those ancient Egyptian role models. During the initial 18 days of the 2011 revolution, women played an indispensable role socially and politically. Some women formed clinics in the square and inside the Omar Makram mosque, whilst others were part of committees that were stationed on the edges of Tahrir Square in order to search protesters for weapons. In the initial phase of the transitional period, they began to be excluded from decision-making and not given the opportunity to play a formal role in the process of reform under way.

"Right after the revolution, it was obvious that women were being excluded. Their voices could not be heard and they started to be marginalised. Hate speech against women spread. Women became scared of losing what they had gained and achieved," said Wahba, who has been involved in several initiatives that aim to promote women's rights and women's representation in the political life post-revolution.

When an advisory committee, the Committee of Wise Men, was formed during the uprising in January 2011 it included only one woman among its 30 members. Just before the country's first free and fair parliamentary elections, the legislative committee of the Shura Council abolished the quota system, which had reserved 64

People's Assembly seats for women. Not surprisingly, then, only eight women were elected to parliament out of 508, compared to 60 women in 2010 before the quota was rendered obsolete. The marginalisation of women manifested itself in different forms before and during President Morsi's rule. Women were excluded from the constitutional drafting process and some political parties have questioned and attempted to tamper with the established elements of women's rights legislation, including divorce and custody laws, protection against female genital mutilation, and limits on age of marriage.

the Shura Council's human rights committee issued a controversial statement implying that women taking part in protests bear the responsibility of being sexually harassed

Meanwhile, the drafters of the new constitution proceeded to place impediments to women's right to speak out and participate in public life. Article 10 of the currently suspended Egyptian constitution states: "The state shall provide free motherhood and childhood services and shall balance between a woman's obligations toward the family and public work. The state shall provide for special care and protection for single mothers, divorced women and widows." Such an article risks confining women solely to the role of carer. "The state's role should be confined to ensuring equality and non-discrimination, without interfering with a women's choices about her life, family, and profession or to justify discrimination on that basis," Human Rights Watch said. Meanwhile, women have won some battles. Opposition to a →

ABOVE: Street artist El Zeft's protest poster supporting women in Egypt

→ proposed controversial clause in the constitution suggesting the equality of men and woman would be subject to the rules of "Islamic jurisprudence" led to the clause being dropped.

However, not one woman was selected to be a state governor, and in February 2013, the Shura Council made the controversial decision of reversing a legal condition requiring female parliamentary candidates to be listed at the top of electoral lists. Women's rights activists deplored this ruling as a serious setback for women's representation in the highest decision-making spheres. They noted that not only men but also the few women sitting at the Shura Council and in parliament maintained a conservative stance.

"Chauvinistic rationalisation is evident among all political parties, including the liberal ones. No real focus is placed on gender and women's issues, and the rise in the heinous sexual assaults and mob attacks, and the non-existent response from the entire society, government and political groups and parties, is a seriously negative sign and even bad omen for what shall come next. Women have been attacked right, left and centre since the start of the revolution – by both state and non-state actors that claimed to call for social justice and equality," said Elmohandes.

Wahba, a founding member of the Egyptian Social Democratic Party, said: "As a young woman involved in politics, it is very difficult to have your voice heard because you are marginalised as a woman and you are marginalised as a young person. Yet I am lucky because in my party we have a very strong women's committee. This is encouraging, but there still is so much to do."

Despite being under-represented in the political arena, women have still been eager to participate in Egypt's post-2011 overhaul, with more than 50 marches organised by women's groups in 2012. However, the increase in sexual violence has undermined such initiatives. Women's symbolic and physical exclusion reached a high point with the escalation of mob attacks on female protesters in and around Tahrir Square.

Tahrir – which means freedom in Arabic – is more than a square, it is the symbol of Egyptian people's voice, especially after Egyptian people united and overthrew Hosni Mubarak's authoritarian regime. Because of this, attempts to ban women from this square symbolically highlight the social and political exclusion of women. While the use of sexual violence as a political tool against women in protests is not a new phenomenon in Egypt, it has escalated. Whether committed by the Mubarak regime, the police, the military, political supporters or thugs, sexual violence and the impunity accompanying it are symptoms of deep-rooted social stigma and prejudice towards women's role in society. In recent mass gatherings and protests of June and July 2013 to oust President Morsi, two organisations, Nazra for Feminist Studies and Operation Anti-Sexual Harassment, documented a total of at least 186 cases ranging from group sexual harassment and assault to violent rape of at least three female protesters.

The phenomenon has been called "sexual terrorism", with rumours of thugs being paid to assault female protesters. The lack of political will to address such a phenomenon and the time it took for public opinion to condemn such practices reveals the degree to which gender equality had increased. Worse, in February 2013, the Shura Council's human rights committee issued a controversial statement implying that women taking part in protests bear the responsibility of being sexually harassed. The most provocative statements described what happened in some demonstrators' tents as "prostitution", while others called on women not to stand among men during protests, or not to go to protests at all.

The tragedy of sexual violence and the former government's response are a reflection of the biggest impediment in any Egyptian woman's life: cultural and societal barriers. Women's marginalisation in politics is complex and cannot be explained only by the removal of quota laws, the lack of female candidates and sexual harassment. Elmohandes says it was not just the authorities that were responsible for women's marginalisation. "People are not open to the idea of the presence of the woman in the public sphere." Despite women's skills and presence in almost all professional sectors, they still face obstacles to being represented in politics, whether in ministerial or mayoral positions. In 2012, Egypt dropped three places on the Global Gender Gap Index, ranking 126 out of 135, as a result of worsening perception of wage equality between women and men for similar work and a decrease in enrolment in secondary education. The report also shows that Egypt ranks tenth from the bottom in female political empowerment.

Legislative change is necessary to protect and empower women, but even with quotas and parity laws, which would promote and advance gender justice, there has to be a true intent to upgrade women's participation and representation in society. This can and has to be done both at the national and local levels.

At the national level, it is possible to launch awareness campaigns and educational tools promoting women's rights, fighting gender violence and nequality. At the local level, community workshops and programmes aimed at increasing women's literacy, economic independence, and self-confidence

Tahrir – which means freedom in Arabic – is more than a square, it is the symbol of Egyptian people's voice, especially after people united and overthrew Hosni Mubarak's authoritarian regime

have already showed results. For example, the Association for the Development and Empowerment of Women (ADEW) has been working on helping women, especially heads of households, learn more about their legal, economic, social, political and cultural rights to give them more power within society.

Women such as Om Ali, a community leader and microcredit recipient in a deprived area on the edge of Cairo, epitomises what a community workshop can achieve. Her story demonstrates the benefits of a bottom-up approach, which can not only empower women, it can be extremely effective in changing social perceptions and strengthening women's voices in the community (see sidebar).

In light of 30 June 2013, many challenges stand in the way of Egyptian women's access to public spaces. According to human →

→ rights defender Ghada Shahbendar, hope lies in the empowerment of not just women, but also young people: "I call 25 January the revolution of youth and women. Egypt has a very young population – average age is 24.5, the majority of Egyptians are under the age of 30 – and that is our demographic gift." Shahbendar believes that the key lies in empowering young women who will be the leaders of tomorrow, while challenging "the very small fraction of Egyptian society resisting change". "I can see it coming," she adds on a positive note. Wahba, the politician, shares Shahbendar's views: "I think it is crucial to empower youth, and when doing so, we need to empower young women, not only young men. Pushing women to the frontlines and making sure that they are represented in all the decision-making places is essential. We need to support women committees in political parties, capacity building, and ensure that they have a voice."

The overthrow of Morsi's government makes things uncertain for women's future. While the newly appointed interim president, Adly Mansour, has chosen few female ministers – the new interim government has three female ministers out of 33 – women need to be further integrated into the new roadmap and not be confined to women's portfolios. It is of paramount importance for women leaders to branch out beyond women-only committees and ministries. At the same time, awareness campaigns and support to women empowerment programmes at the community level can make a difference. "My hope is to have a constitution that guarantees women's rights, to have more women ministers, more women governors, more women holding responsible positions at the local level, women mayors and at town councils, but also more women within internal political parties, quotas, and more women being heads of political parties. I see the increasing political participation after the revolution as a window of opportunity," insists Dina Wahba. "Repre-

senting women from all sectors and classes, all religions, in politics is crucial."

Guaranteeing women access to freedom of expression and protecting their participation in public and political spaces is vital both to support the Egyptian transition and development process and as a development goal in its own right. "The struggle of women in Egypt continues on several fronts, and the struggle keeps increasing every day," said Elmohandes. X

©Melody Patry and Rasha Mohamed
www.indexoncensorship.org

Melody Patry is advocacy officer at Index on Censorship and **Rasha Mohamed** is the head of the international relations division at the Arab Penal Reform Organisation in Cairo

Om Ali's story

As I entered Om Ali's home, two rooms on the second floor of a small cement building on the edge of Cairo, she apologised for the mess and timidly adjusted her scarf. She started making tea, boiling water on a portable gas stove and lining up glasses on a dented aluminium tray. As we finished our cup s of tea, Om Ali told me her story. She spoke in a calm and resolute manner: "Before this I was doing nothing, I didn't used to do anything, I was just sitting like this all day, without thinking, waiting for my husband to come back from work, because he made the money."

Om Ali was one of many who worked with the Association for the Development and Empowerment of Women (ADEW), a local women's NGO that teaches women social empowerment skills. Prior to this work, her life plan looked to be sketched out for her by society and her poverty. It was expected that she would become a wife and that this would be her main function in life. But then she learned to read, thanks to ADEW.

Her relationship with her family, and most importantly with her husband, changed as she learnt skills that could help her make money: "Before if we clashed or if we had a misunderstanding, I had to conform and I had to submit because he was the man of the house and I couldn't do anything. But after I joined the literacy and micro credit programme, we had to be equal."

He told her: "You earn money, I earn money, you're educated, I'm educated." "Now at least I can educate my girls, at least I can read, at least I am able to prepare my girls to be married," Om Ali explained, while showing me photos of the family wedding on the wall.

Om Ali, who lives in Gamaa Amr, was one of ADEW's first beneficiaries 25 years ago. She attended literacy courses, obtained identity papers and participated in various workshops on boosting self-esteem, improving decision-making and negotiation skills, whilst encouraging participation in public life. She also joined ADEW's micro credit programme, like many other women in her neighbourhood. "At least now we can read, we understand, we know what is going on in the world. At least now we're able to deal with one another, we're able to deal with people, I now know how to communicate. This is something we weren't able to do. And now I am a micro credit facilitator, I am not only a recipient. I am respected in the community. When people have problems, they come to see me, they listen to me, I have influence."

Om Ali is proud of her achievements and now identifies herself as a "head of household". Economic independence, literacy and self-confidence contributed to raise Om Ali's interest in and access to politics. "You know in Egypt before the [2011] revolution when you wanted to vote, you had to have a voting ID, not just your ID. Back then, ADEW took us to the police station to issue our voting ID. I was able to choose." Other women like Om Ali have benefited from this bottom-up approach, which aims to empower women to become active participants in their own development and informed decision-makers in their home and communities.

Part of this approach at the community level is also about changing misconceptions about women's roles. ADEW project manager Sarah Hani explains how women find ways around family restrictions and social constraints to attend ADEW's programmes, such as Arab Women Speak Out (AWSO): "Some women do not tell their husbands what kind of programme this is, they just say it's a purely educational one, mentioning nothing about the social empowerment aspect of it. Others tell their husbands a very brief idea on what they take in the classes so that their husbands are reassured and know what their wives are doing while they're not at home. Others try to pass on to their husbands what they learn from the lessons, to keep their husbands on the same page as them."

The idea of women being the main breadwinner of their households is still sensitive, especially after the revolution, when many businesses have shut down, and many men have lost their jobs. As Om Ali said: "Nowadays in this area, it's the women who really make the income. Especially if you get out in the neighbourhood in the morning you find so many women out in the streets selling breakfast for kids, for parents, and now if you go out in the streets you find mostly men sitting in the coffee shops, drinking tea, smoking shisha and whatever. Now it's the time for women, they're the ones who have a job, because of the micro credit programme."

Hani emphasises why it is important for women's voices to be heard at home – and in order to be heard in parliament, especially after the 2011 revolution. "These communities' sense of public participation started to rise, they started becoming more engaged in public life, caring to go to vote because they were economically affected, and that's when those people feel the sense that they need to take part in the country's public life." Supporting women's rights and empowerment at the community level can be just as powerful, as it helps create a necessary foundation for amplifying women's voices in Egypt's public spaces.

Melody Patry

Changing the script

42(3): 25/28 | DOI: 10.1177/0306422013503276

Using a soap opera and storytelling workshops, Theatre for a Change breaks down barriers between communities in Malawi and Ghana. **Natasha Schmidt** talks to founder Patrick Young

IN MALAWI, WOMEN aged between 15 and 24 are five times more likely to contract HIV than men in the same age group. Frequently, police are involved in the intimidation and harassment of vulnerable women. Sex workers are attacked. In Ghana, despite considerable economic growth and a marked decline in the number of people contracting HIV, many people do not feel do not feel their lives have improved, with extreme poverty affecting 30 per cent of the population, high unemployment among young people and uneven levels of education across the country.

So how can these groups make their voices heard and transform their lives?

For Patrick Young, director of Theatre for a Change (TFAC), an NGO that works with some of the most disadvantaged groups in these countries, it's about telling stories – and choosing which audience will hear them. Using legislative or participatory theatre, inspired by Brazilian Augusto Boal's Theatre of the Oppressed, the project uses performance techniques to bring about changes in society. Tapping into the important role that oral traditions play in many African countries, it aims to equip socially and economically marginalised communities with communication skills and knowledge to transform their lives. Legislative theatre encourages participants to recount negative experiences by re-enacting them, addressing their

grievances directly to people who have been at least partly responsible for these encounters, such as police or politicians, and it invites those responsible to take part too. It's a powerful tool, says Young, because one of its key principles is the belief that people are "experts in their own lives", that no one else is qualified to tell their story. Among participants are groups that have a big impact on sections of society but who are also vulnerable in some way – for example, the police in Malawi, who have the second highest risk of contracting HIV, or teachers, the third highest risk group. How these groups interact with →

BELOW: Interactive theatre performance with schoolchildren, Malawi

→ the stories or "performances" by other more marginalised groups can be crucial in changing how these people interact with one another, and can have a knock-on effect in wider society. In one example, local police began to change their institutional behaviour towards women in sex work, treating them with respect and not making assumptions. Minimising the risk of contracting HIV is one of the founding objectives of TFAC. It's a complex issue in Malawi because some of the most powerful sections of society – including the police and teachers – are also the most vulnerable.

Using a technique known as "touch tagging", in which participants physically tag one another in order to highlight a particular conflict and express how it might be resolved, TFAC helps people examine hostilities – for example, between sex workers

People address their grievances directly to police or politicians

and the police force in the case of Malawi. By inviting participants to play active roles, an important aspect of legislative theatre, policemen can briefly "become" sex workers and vice versa.

In Malawi, TFAC also runs a hugely successful interactive radio soap opera – with an audience of around 500,000 people – which takes as its theme some of the most pressing issues facing these communities today. The programme encourages listeners to call in and participate directly with the conflict being performed.

In one project, sex workers acted out their experiences to the police and local decision-makers and later went on to present their story to the much wider civil society sector, including the UN. A group in Malawi took their story to the Malawian Parliament in 2010. Initially, politicians were hesitant to acknowledge what they were being told

– details about violence and harassment suffered by sex workers – but the participatory, theatrical component to the project makes it not only a neutral way of diffusing resistance but also a hugely entertaining, even fun, one, Young says. The performance didn't result in a legislative change, but it did challenge MPs to confront their prejudices about women and sex work. So, Young says, "we see very simple human dynamics being taken into a legislative and policy-making forum." Malawi's media responded, too, by asking whether sex work could be legalised or decriminalised, and opening up a debate that had not been part of public discourse before.

While the performed stories are never written down, they are always created by those who have lived the experience, and initiated by facilitators working in the local languages in Malawi and Ghana, Chichewa and Ga, as well as in English. TFAC employs a three-part strategy (or theory of change) in which an individual changes how they see themselves and how he or she views their ability to assert particular rights. Young says that what's key is building communication skills, leading to an ability to negotiate and be assertive. When a group advocates for their rights "using their words, using their voices," Young says, change at a societal level is realised. Facilitators witness groups becoming more cohesive and working together. Increasingly, these changes have a wider reach; TFAC currently runs workshops across the whole of Malawi with the police and the army. They've also seen change in the education system and attitudes around it. It's about people being able to directly advocate their rights – to refuse unwanted sex, to report on exploitation, to practise freedom of expression in an incredibly powerful way. Young warns of the dangers of taking these very unique stories out of the hands of the people telling the story. "We're interested in equipping people with skills to advocate for themselves," says Young. "For a lot of

ABOVE: Participants at a workshop in Ghana

people who are marginalised, the written word is not necessarily the most comfortable one."

In both Ghana and Malawi, there are perceived and very real limitations to the right to freedom of expression, Young says. But the participatory approach to performance provides a culturally acceptable platform for people without power to talk to those in power without feeling threatened. Because the oral tradition is socially acceptable and familiar, it doesn't pose a threat to the status quo. "The right to freedom of expression is being claimed, but not in an explicit way," he says. Many lines of power or societal

norms can be subverted by powerful cultural traditions, which involve changing roles or rebalancing levels of power within a liminal space for a period of time. "All cultures have those moments of transformation, like Mardi Gras, where the weak are strong and the strong are made weak," Young says. In Malawi, Gule Wamkulu, a tradition where young men dress up or disguise themselves using paint, feathers and masks, serves as a space of transformation; men feel they have licence to cause trouble and step out of their normal lives. When it's over, they take off their masks and go back to work and resume their normal lives. "Our method- →

→ ology taps into that recognisable arena and that recognisable space where change is allowed and expression is permitted," he adds. But he also points out that TFAC does not want those who have been disempowered to dominate the discussion, to be in a position of power, drowning out other voices. "What we're looking for is balance," he says. "We try not to come to a situation of injustice with an agenda." Collaboration is key.

Ghana is widely seen as one of the most progressive countries in the African sub-continent, in terms of economic growth, promoting democratic values and supporting human rights. So how does this relative success feed in to TFAC's work in the country – and what are the limitations? "Ghana has a longer history of independence than Malawi, so it has a much stronger sense of freedom and freedom of expression," says Young. "Ghanaians are very confident about their right to express themselves. But there's a long way to go because that's truer for some people than others. If you're poor and female, then the opportunity to express yourself is significantly reduced in both Ghana and Malawi. ... There's still a lot to do in terms of gender and power – and freedom of expression." X

©Natasha Schmidt
www.indexoncensorship.org

Natasha Schmidt is deputy editor of Index on Censorship magazine

Moving towards inequality

42(3): 29/32 | DOI: 10.1177/0306422013500186

In China, social benefits are tied an antiquated system of household registration that restricts benefits to the place where people were born. As hundreds of millions leave the countryside to seek employment in the cities, they are left without official jobs, legal protection or school places for their children. **Jemimah Steinfeld** and **Hannah Leung** report

WHEN LIANG HONG returned to her hometown of Liangzhuang, Henan province, in 2011, she was instantly struck by how many of the villagers had left, finding work in cities all across China. It was then that she decided to chronicle the story of rural migrants. During the next two years she visited over 10 cities, including Beijing, and interviewed around 340 people. Her resultant book, Going Out of Liangzhuang, which was published in early 2013, became an overnight success. In March it topped the Most Quality Book List compiled by the book channel of leading web portal Sina.

Liang's book is unique, providing a rare opportunity for migrants to narrate their stories. They have been described as *san sha* (scattered sand) because they lack collective strength and power to change their circumstance. "They are invisible members of society," Liang told Index. "They have no agency. There is a paradox here. On one hand, villagers are driven away from their homes to find jobs and earn money. But on the other hand, the cities they go to do not have a place for them."

The central reason? China's *hukou*, or household registration system. The *hukou*, which records a person's family history, has existed for around 2,000 years, originally to keep track of who belonged to which family. Then, in 1958 under Mao Zedong, the *hukou* started to be used to order and control society. China's population was divided into rural and urban communities. The idea was that farmers could generate produce and live off it, while excess would feed urban factory workers, who in turn would receive significantly better benefits of education, health care and pensions. But the economic reforms starting in the late 1970s created pressure to encourage migration from rural to urban areas. Today 52 per cent of the population live in a metropolis, with a predicted rise to 66 per cent by 2020.

In this context authorities have debated making changes to the system, or eradicating it altogether. In the 1990s some cities, including Shanghai, Shenzhen and Guangzhou, started to allow people to acquire a local *hukou* if they bought property in the city →

→ or invested large quantities of money. In Beijing specifically, a local *hukou* can be acquired by joining the civil service, working for a state-owned company or ascending to the top ranks of the military.

The scope of these exceptions remains small, though, and an improvement is more a rhetorical statement than a reality. "China has been talking about reforming the *hukou* system for the last 20 years. Most *hukou* reform measures so far are quite limited and tend to favour the rich and the highly educated. They have not changed much of the substance," University of Washington professor Kam Wing Chan, a specialist in Chinese urbanisation and the hukou, told Index.

Thus some 260 million Chinese migrants live as second-class citizens. Shanghai, for example, has around 10 million migrant workers who cannot access the same social services as official citizens.

Of the social services, education is where the *hukou* system particularly stings. Fully-funded schooling and entrance exams are only offered in the parents' hometown, where standards are lower and competition for university places higher. Charitable schools have sprung up, but they are often subject to government crackdown. Earlier this year one district in Beijing alone pledged to close all its migrant schools.

It's not just in terms of social services that migrants suffer. Many bosses demand a local *hukou* and exploit those without. A labour contract law passed in 2008 remains largely ineffective and the majority of migrants work without contracts. Indeed, it was only in 2003 that migrants could join the All-China Federation of Trade Unions (ACFTU), and to this day the ACFTU does little to recruit them.

The main official channel to voice discontent is to petition local government. Failing that, these ex-rural residents could organise protests or strikes. Given that neither free speech nor the right to assembly is protected in China, all of these options remain largely ineffective, and relatively unlikely. In a rare case in Yunnan province, southwest China, tourism company Xinhua Shihaizi owed RMB8 million (US$1.3 million) to 500 migrant workers for a construction project. With no one fighting their battle, children joined parents and held up signs in public. In this case the company was fined. Other instances are less successful, with reports of violence either at the hands of police or thugs hired by employers being rife.

"Many of them fight or rebel in small ways to get limited justice, because they cannot fight the system on a larger scale," noted Liang. "For example, my uncle told me that he would steal things from the factory he worked at to sell later. This was a way of getting back at his boss, who was a cruel man." In lieu of institutional support, NGOs step in. Civil society groups have been legalised since 1994, providing they register with a government sponsor. This is not always easy and migrant workers' organisations in particular are subject to close monitoring and control. Subsequently only around 450,000 non-profits are legally registered in China, with an estimated one million more unregistered.

But since Xi Jinping became general secretary of the Communist Party of China in March, civil society groups have grown in number. Index spoke to Geoff Crothall from China Labour Bulletin, a research and rights project based in Hong Kong. They work with several official migrant NGOs in mainland China. Crothall said that while these groups have experienced harassment in the past, there has been nothing serious of late.

Migrants themselves are also changing their approach. "Young migrant workers all have cell phones and are interested in technology and know how to use social media. So certainly things such as social media feed Weibo could be a way for them to express themselves," Liang explained.

ABOVE: Rural migrants from Hebei province on a street corner in Beijing

It's not just in terms of new technology that action is being taken. In Pi village, just outside of Beijing, former migrant Sun Heng has established a museum on migrant culture and art. Despite being closely monitored, with employees cautioned by officials against talking to foreigners, it remains open and offers aid to migrants on the side.

There are other indications that times are changing. China's new leaders have signalled plans to amend the hukou system later this year. Whether this is once again hot air is hard to say. But they are certainly allowing more open conversation about hukou policy reform. Just prior to the release of Liang's book, in December 2012 the story of 15-year-old Zhan Haite became headline news when Zhan, her father and → other migrants took to Shanghai's People's Square with a banner reading: "Love the motherland, love children", in response to not being allowed to continue her education in the city.

Initially there was a backlash. The family were evicted from their house and her father was imprisoned for several weeks. Hostility also came from Shanghai's hukou holders, who are anxious to keep privileges to themselves. Then something remarkable happened: Haite was invited to write an op-ed for national newspaper China Daily, signalling a potential change in tack.

It's about time. The *hukou* system, which has been labelled by some as a form of apartheid, is indefensible on both a moral and economic level in today's China. Its continuation stands to threaten the stability of the nation, as it aggravates the gulf between haves and have-nots. Reform in smaller cities is a step in the right direction, but it's in the biggest cities where these gaps are most pronounced. And as the migration of thousands of former agricultural workers to the cities continues, that division is set to deepen if nothing else is done. ☒

©Jemimah Steinfeld and Hannah Leung
www.indexoncensorship.org

Jemimah Steinfeld worked as a reporter in Beijing for CNN, Huffington Post and Time Out Beijing. At present she is writing a book on Chinese youth culture
Hannah Leung is an American-born Chinese freelance journalist who has spent the past four years in China. She is currently living in Beijing

Portrait of a paperless and powerless worker

....

Deng Qing Ning, 37, has worked as an *ayi* in Beijing for the last seven years. At the moment she charges RMB15 (US$2.40) per hour for her routine cleaning services, though she is thinking of increasing her rates to RMB20 to match the market. She hasn't yet, for fear that current clients will resist.

The word *ayi* in Mandarin can be used as a generic term for auntie, but it also refers to a cleaner or maid. Most *ayi* perform a gamut of chores, from taking care of children to cleaning, shopping and cooking.

While *ayi* in cities like Hong Kong are foreign live-in workers with a stipulated monthly minimum wage (currently HK$3920, US$505), domestic help in China hails from provinces outside of the cities they work. In places like Beijing and Shanghai, the hourly services of non-contractual *ayi* cost the price of a cheap coffee.

Deng's story is typical of many *ayi* who service the homes of Beijingers. She was born in 1976 in a village outside Chongqing, in China's southwestern Sichuan province, where her parents remain. She came to Beijing in 2006 to join her husband. He had moved up north to find work in construction after the two wed in 2004.

"In Beijing, there are more regulations and more opportunities", she said, explaining why they migrated to China's capital. "Everyone leaves my hometown. Only kids and elders remain."

When she arrived in Beijing, she immediately found work as an *ayi* through an agency. The agency charged customers RMB25 (US$4) per hour for cleaning services and would pocket RMB10, alongside a deposit. One day, at one of the houses Deng was assigned, her client offered to pay her directly, instead of going through a middleman. The set-up was mutually beneficial.

"When I discovered there was the opportunity to break free, I took it", she said, adding that many of the cleaning companies rip off their workers.

One perk of being an *ayi* is Deng's ability to take care of her daughter. When her daughter was younger and needed supervision, she joined her mother on the job. Now that her daughter is older, Deng is able to pick her up from school.

But this is where the benefits end. Her family does not receive any social welfare. Not having a Beijing hukou means not qualifying for free local education, which makes her nine-year-old daughter a heavy financial burden. Many Beijing schools do not accept migrant children at all.

Aware of these hardships in advance, Deng and her husband were still insistent on bringing their daughter with them to the city, instead of leaving her behind to be raised by grandparents, which is a situation many children of migrant workers face.

"The education in Beijing is better than back home," she explained. Her daughter attends a local migrant school, a spot secured after they bargained for her to take the place of their nephew. Her brother-in-law's family had just moved back home because their children kept falling ill.

Deng has to cover some of the fees and finds the urban education system unfair, but she highlights how difficult it is to voice these frustrations.

"Many Beijing kids do not even have good academic records. Our children may be better than theirs. But they take care of Beijingers first."

She wishes the government would establish more schools; her daughter's class size has increased three times during the school year. Again, there is nothing they can do and few people she can talk to, she says. It's not like they have the political or business *guangxi* (connections) or know a local teacher who can get their daughter admission anywhere else.

Deng's younger brother, born in 1986, followed his sister to Beijing five years ago and found employment as a construction worker. Three years back Deng received a dreaded phone call. Her brother had been in a serious accident on a construction site, where he tripped over an electrical wire and tumbled down a flight of stairs. He was temporarily blinded due to an injury that impaired his nerves.

The construction site had violated various safety laws. To the family's relief, the supervisor of the project footed the hospital bills in Beijing's Jishuitan Hospital, which amounted to more than RMB20,000 (US$3,235). During this time, Deng had to curb her working hours to attend to her brother, but she felt grateful given the possibility of a worse scenario. Her brother's vision never fully recovered and he returned to their hometown shortly after.

Deng is looking forward to the time when they can all reunite, hopefully once her daughter reaches secondary school. More opportunities are developing in her hometown, which makes a return to Sichuan and relief from her paperless status much more appealing.

Protesters and poorest create own news media

42(3): 33/36 | DOI: 10.1177/0306422013501769

During Brazil's largest protests in years, small news collectives and activists took to the streets to report. Whether it's community radio or blogs covering topics the mainstream media ignore, the country's poorest communities are making their voices heard, **Ronaldo Pelli** reports

FROM THE SUBURBS of São Paulo to the poorest favelas in Rio de Janeiro, ordinary people are transforming Brazil's media landscape. As with the Arab Spring, Spain's protest group, *Indignados*, the Occupy movement and Istanbul's Taksim Square protests, the internet and social media played a central role in Brazil's June 2013 protests. Demonstrators used Facebook and You-Tube to organise and broadcast. Initially the protests were against the rise in public transport fares. Next came a large agenda of complaints, from the costs of the 2014 FIFA World Cup to corruption among politicians and lack of investment in public education and healthcare. Hundreds of thousands of people took part; on 20 June alone, more than a million people in dozens of towns across the country came out on the streets.

According to a survey by Brazil's most prominent research institute, Ibope, 91 per cent of the protesters heard about the movement via the internet, with 77 per cent using Facebook. Some analysts viewed the protests as a result of Brazil's growth in GDP and recent improvement in some social indicators. With more of the population in education, there may well be more critics voicing opinions about politicians.

These protests – and the way they were reported and organised – did not happen in isolation. They emerged from a burgeoning new Brazil, where increasing numbers of

The traditional media depict poor neighbourhoods as the dark side of the city, as everything rich people do not want to be

people can make their voices heard. Recent improvements in the country have made this possible, particularly under the presidency of Dilma Da Silva-Rousseff. The previous president, Fernando Henrique Cardoso, managed to get high rates of inflation under control and stabilised the currency when he was finance minister in 1993, making Brazil a more fertile place for not only economic growth but free expression and social change. →

ABOVE: Summer 2013 saw some of the largest protests in years, primarily organised online

→ The group Midia Ninja was launched on 13 June, when protests first kicked off in São Paulo. "We decided to go to the streets to cover it," says journalist Bruno Torturra, one of the founders of the collective. Their aim was to cover protests around the country. Midia Ninja built their newsroom at the beginning of July; a website hosting videos of protests (http://www.postv.org/) followed. "We could see that the traditional model of journalism is in crisis," Torturra says. They used Facebook to publicise their coverage – and it worked. They posted one request for voluntary support on social media and they received more than 1,500 offers of help from more than 100 Brazilian cities.

The Committee for the Democratization of Computing (CDI) is one of the fruits of this new Brazil, born after 20 years of dictatorship, and after ten years trying to find its own path, and voice. When the organisation founded its first centre in Rio's Dona Marta favela in 1995, the aim was to bring computer access to everyone. At the time most people on low incomes hadn't seen a keyboard, a computer mouse, let alone had internet access in their homes. Today, CDI's expertise has reached more than 1.5 million.

CDI's chief executive, Marcel Fukayama, says that the goals of the organisation have continued to follow the changing needs and will of the people. "We believe that the protests across the country were 100 per cent connected with our vision," he says.

These days, it seems, people want more than consumerism. They want a say in their country. Computers – and specifically the internet and social media sites – are effective tools for making this possible.

CDI's Fukayama explains that its actual main objective is to "transform lives and develop communities. Transformation is our responsibility, not government's or business," he says. They employ five steps to help small communities use technology to improve their lives. According to Fukayama, CDI must be invited by a community representative to set up a centre. First CDI staff survey the neighbourhood in order to understand its environment. They identify problems and possible solutions. They then create an action plan, execute it and evaluate the whole process. This strategy seems to be successful: CDI is active in 13 countries and 780 communities around the world, from England to Ecuador. In 2012, there were 92,084 direct beneficiaries.

In response to critics, some of whom argue that CDI is simply about making money and that the positive social outcomes are just a by-product, Fukayama says, "Some people's visions are stuck in the past. They think that to deal with traditional companies is awkward, they say that you cannot have profit, you cannot focus on the outcome." He adds that the old, outdated model of the

NGO had to change, particularly following the recent economic crisis in Western countries, after which companies reorganised their budgets around social responsibility. "We don't teach youngsters how to push a button, we try to explain how this button can change a life and a community."

According to Abong, the Brazilian association of NGOs, there are almost 291,000 different non-profit private foundations in the country. One of the best-known organisations focusing on social issues is the *Observatório de Favelas* (Favelas Observatory). In 2012, it published a report looking at alternative media in poor communities in Rio, revealing that 104 different media initiatives operated in these areas. The report also aimed to understand how inhabitants of these areas see and represent themselves.

Eight corporations control about 80 per cent of all of the traditional media in Brazil. They mainly depict poor neighbourhoods as the dark side of the city, as everything rich people do not want to be. Observatório's report argued that these big corporations still have massive control of how favelas are represented – but they are no longer the only ones reporting on these communities. Journalists from the traditional media were also targeted in some of the recent protests in São Paulo and Rio. In one incident, rioters set fire to one van from a TV channel. In Rio, reporters were expelled from rallies. It seems people want to hear their voices reported in a different way.

People from favelas write blogs, produce newspapers, magazines and websites, as well as radio and television programmes. Rocinha.org, based in the biggest slum in Latin America, has almost 900,000 visits per month, with numbers increasing all the time. According to the site, at the time of its launch in 2006 most online news about the favela was linked to violence or drug dealing. "It was necessary to confront it, and give the other side of the story", the website states. As a result, the NGO, the website and

a strong commitment to the community it focused on was born.

For Mídia Ninja, it's about going to the streets and working rather than staying in an office, planning what to do. According to Torturro, the group still doesn't know how to survive financially, but they refuse to worry about it at the moment. Their reporting has been celebrated. For their involvement in the action, sometimes very energetic, they have been accused of being biased. "We are trying to change the journalism standard image from the cold neutrality to a passionate objectivity," he says.

New voices have also been amplified through the organisation Oi Kabum, a joint

We don't teach youngsters how to push a button, we try to explain how this button can change a life and a community

project between Cecip, a NGO linked to alternative media in Brazil, and Oi, one of the biggest telecommunications companies in the country. The organisation has help set up schools that specialise in technology in four regions: Rio, Belo Horizonte (in the rich southeast region), Salvador and Recife (in the not-so-well-developed northeast region).

One of their teachers, Lorenzo Aldé, agrees that the internet is not a problem for those who live in Brazil's biggest cities. He teaches 90 students from 16 to 21 from poor neighbourhoods. All of them have some way of connecting to the internet and have access to a digital camera. According to Aldé, the message to students is: "You do whatever you want to do here."

Under the Oi Kabum scheme, teenagers attend classes focusing on video, photography, graphic design or computer graphics from 8am to midday for 18 months. The school enrols one group of students per session, in order to give ample attention →

→ and focus to every single student. "They use their identities, their values, their cultural references, even their troubles' as subject matter for their work," says Aldé.

The programme started in 2009, and its first students graduated in 2011. Already, they have success stories to tell. Former students are now working with renowned producers or famous bands and passing on their knowledge to children from other poor communities.

What Mídia Ninja, Oi Kabum, CDI and other groups are doing is more or less what most of the protesters have been trying to do on Brazilian streets. They are sending a message: Brazilian people don't want just a computer anymore. They want their citizenship back, in all that entails. And they will scream until their voices are heard. X

©Ronaldo Pelli
www.indexoncensorship.org

Ronaldo Pelli is a freelance journalist based in Rio de Janeiro. He writes regularly for *Revista de História da Biblioteca Nacional*

Pride and prejudices

42(3): 37/39 | DOI: 10.1177/0306422013500410

Rights and reality come into conflict for South African gay community, says **Natasha Joseph**

DISCUSSING LESBIAN, GAY, bisexual, transgendered, intersex and queer rights (LGBTI) in South Africa is deeply contradictory. On the one hand, the country boasts some of the most progressive LGBTI rights in the world – from its constitution, protecting people from discrimination on the grounds of sexual orientation, to legalised same sex unions. Cape Town is a popular holiday destination for the international LGBTI community, as well as being the centre for the "pink rand". In fact South Africa leads on the African continent when it comes to LGBTI rights.

But this idyllic picture is just one side of the coin: on the flipside, South Africa is nonetheless a very dangerous place for those who identify as LGBTI. Particularly vulnerable are black lesbians, because, in South Africa, black women tend to be victims of crime more than any other group, and because black lesbian sexuality is considered to be an affront to disenfranchised, angry men of the country's townships. These women are frequently raped, often by gangs of men, and their murders tend to be brutal – in one recent case on Johannesburg's East Rand a 25-year-old woman, Duduzile Zozo, was found dead in a neighbour's garden with a toilet brush shoved into her vagina.

Gay men are also targeted. A spate of murders in Johannesburg, Durban and more recently, Cape Town, has drawn attention to the vulnerability of middle-aged, mostly white gay men who are killed and robbed in their own homes. There is much speculation in the local media as to whether these are hate crimes or the work of a syndicate of robbers who kill their victims to dispose of any witnesses.

Homosexuality is often decried by South African religious and traditional leaders as "unholy" or "unAfrican". This, combined with a dearth of political will to really tackle

A group of LGBTI activists stepped into the vacuum – and went about canvassing community opinions in a modern and fascinating way

hate crimes linked to sexuality, means the progressive laws in place in South Africa are often little more than paper tigers in many sections of society.

So, which spaces are opening up for LGBTI men and women and those who identify as intersex or queer in a country whose attitude teeters between progressive and deeply hostile? The answer lies, at least in part, online. The 2012 Johannesburg Pride march was marred by clashes between the →

ABOVE: Tussles for control of the Johannesburg Pride parade took place last year

→ white, middle-class crowd that traditionally attends this event and a small but vocal group of predominantly black women activists who were determined to draw attention to the murder of black lesbians.

Just over half of those who could access the internet do so using their mobile phones, Statistics SA reported

A video of Pride participants – members of the organising committee – angrily and aggressively confronting the activists, was uploaded onto YouTube; people tweeted about the clashes and the story made national headlines. Not long afterwards, it emerged that the existing

Johannesburg Pride committee was disbanding. A group of LGBTI activists stepped into the vacuum – and went about canvassing community opinions in a modern and fascinating way. They set up a Facebook page, encouraged people to offer their ideas about how a new and re-imagined Pride could be set up and run, and then held public meetings at which these suggestions were discussed. The new committee has now established an official Johannesburg Pride Facebook page and website, where they explain that the new event will highlight the juxtaposition of South Africa's progressive values with its deeply hostile reality.

The Johannesburg Pride example suggests that the internet offers a democratic space in which different voices and views can step into debates they have not previously been able to access. But there are flaws inherent in this approach. One young man I spoke to, who followed the debates on the original Facebook page and attended several community meetings about the event, said he had always thought of the internet and social media as completely democratic spaces. When he got involved in this process, though, his attitude shifted. He identified access as a huge obstacle to really diversifying online spaces. "In almost every case … you'll find that access to these opportunities and possibilities is constrained by things like race and class," he told me in a Facebook chat.

Indeed, access to the internet, while on the increase in South Africa, is still minimal. The most recent Census data, released in November last year, revealed that less than half of South African households have access to the internet. The majority of those who could access the internet (and 35.2% have web access in South Africa) did so using their mobile phones, Statistics SA reported.

There's another problem, too, in a country like South Africa. Its Gini coefficient – the most commonly used measure of income inequality – is among the highest in the world, marking it out as a deeply unequal society. And if "real life" spaces are dominated by largely white, middle-class men and (to a lesser extent) women, why should things be any different online?

There's also the issue of silencing, whether it be direct or indirect. According to the activist I spoke to on Facebook, censorship and self-censorship come into play "because of the extent of your social capital, your perceived level of education (read: whiteness) and a whole lot of other things tied to the material and structural realities of this country," he wrote.

During the online discussion before the new Pride structure was established, as well as at subsequent community meetings, he noticed that some black men and women did not feel comfortable contributing their thoughts or ideas. This wasn't just because they didn't believe their spoken or written English was "good enough" for the more vocal members of the group. Instead, it was the historical disadvantage that plays out every day in South Africa moving into new spaces – those who spoke "well", or perhaps just loudest, dominated the discussion.

Despite these challenges, it seems likely that online spaces will come to be occupied more frequently by more the marginalised members of the greater LGBTI community. Government control of the internet in South Africa is minimal, so the country does not face the same restrictions on freedom of expression and association as is the case in some neighbouring states.

And, despite new media transforming too slowly for many people's liking, some sites – particularly blogs – may provide a safe space for those who wish to draw attention to underreported issues concerning the LGBTI community. One example is photographer and activist Zanele Muholi's blog, Inkanyiso, which documents the stories of black lesbians who have been the victims of "corrective" rape, designed to "cure" them of their sexuality. Here, women are able to tell their stories in a safe and supportive space – an excellent example of how powerful the internet can be for LGBTI people in South Africa. ☒

©Natasha Joseph
www.indexoncensorship.org

Natasha Joseph is a journalist based in South Africa (@tashjoeza)

Invisible women

42(3): 40/45 | DOI: 10.1177/0306422013500738

For women, feeling comfortable walking across an urban street is not just about safety, but also laying claim to full citizenship of Indian cities, argue **Shilpa Phadke, Shilpa Ranade** and **Sameera Khan**

THE DECEMBER 2012 Delhi rape case and the subsequent spate of reportage of similar cases across the country have once again brought to the foreground the spectre of violence that looms over women in public spaces. In all forms of public fora, from television and the print media, to debates in colleges, the question of safety of women in our public spaces is being discussed. While, on the one hand, demands for stronger legal structures and effective security measures are being made by the state, on the other hand, the policing of girls and women of all ages by themselves and by those around them has acquired an unprecedented justification.

Unfortunately, then, violence becomes the only language in which one can engage with questions of gender in public spaces, a situation which does nothing to further women's rights to access public space. This single-minded focus on the dangers to women in public space contradicts two well documented facts: one, that more women face violence in private spaces than in public spaces, and two, that more men than women are attacked in public. It is worth rehearsing the argument we made in our book, Why Loiter? Women and Risk on Mumbai Streets: that we need to move beyond the struggle against violence and articulate women's →

ABOVE: Women commuters travel into central Mumbai in a women-only train compartment

Credit: Navesh Chitrakar/Reuters

→ right to the city in terms of the quest for pleasure. Since conditional protection brings only surveillance and control for women, in order to claim the right to public space women must claim the right to risk. To do this we need to redefine our understanding of violence in relation to public space, to see not sexual assault but the denial of access to public space as the worst possible outcome for women.

Most women's toilets close at 9pm, sending the clear message that women are not expected to – and not supposed to – be out in public at night

The desire to access the city for pleasure is not a new one. But for women the desire to be "flaneurs" or "flaneuses" is fraught with obstacles. Among these are ideological obstacles with regard to the "proper" place of women, and material obstacles emanating from the lack of adequate infrastructure such as to facilitate access to wandering in the city. Drawing from our research on women and public spaces in Mumbai, in this article we focus on infrastructure that facilitates access, arguing that while women must have the right to risk, risk should be a matter of choice and not imposed on women through inadequate or short-sighted planning. The right to pleasure, by default, must include the right against violence, in the shape of infrastructure such as transport, street lighting, public toilets and policies that recognise people's fundamental right to access public space. Demanding the right to pleasure does not absolve the city administration of the responsibility of providing these facilities.

Public spaces and infrastructure are usually designed for an abstract generic user. In the context of an ideology that deems women's proper place to be at home, this imagined neutral user of public facilities and infrastructure is invariably male. Not just gender, but all manner of politics – class, caste, religious and sexual, as also physical ability – are part of imagining this "neutral" user. In Mumbai, the prototype user then is not just male but also middle or upper class, Hindu, upper caste, able-bodied and heterosexual. Others who use these spaces and infrastructure just have to adjust and make do with what they get. So the physically challenged have to make do without access to most public transport facilities; the old have to make do with negotiating the high steps of subways and footbridges; the poor have to adjust to paying up for public spaces they once had for free; the lower castes and Muslims have to be content with being allowed just the margins; the gays and lesbians have to pretend to be invisible; and women have to learn extreme bladder control and to negotiate dark streets and unfriendly parks. Infrastructure that privileges the needs of one group stands to reinforce the status quo and promotes an unfair hierarchy.

A default response from decision-makers when the provision of adequate infrastructure for women is discussed, is that there aren't that many women in public spaces in the first place. So the argument, for example, is that there are very few public toilets open at night because there aren't so many women out in public at that time. However, if women users were to be asked this question, they might invert the equation and argue that the lack of public toilets makes it even harder to access public space at night. Changing attitudes may take time, but the provision of infrastructure can be a simple one-time administrative policy decision, which reinforces the point that women belong in public space.

A successful example of this in Mumbai is the presence of reserved compartments for women in local trains. These compartments clearly enshrine their right to be in that public space and one cannot overstate the extent to which this simple provision has affected women's ability to commute and therefore access education and employment in the city. If Mumbai women are seen as being privileged in their mobility in the city compared to women in other Indian cities, the city's functioning and expansive public transport can definitely claim some credit for this.

On the other hand, an exemplification of difference-blind design is the public toilet. As if the lack of adequate numbers of toilets in the city was not enough, the facilities provided for women are usually less than half of those for men. Moreover, the design of facilities in toilets that do exist also fails to provide for the specific needs of women. Most "ladies" toilets are dark and unfriendly and designed with minimal thought to women's particular biological and social needs. Women use toilets more frequently and for longer than men. They often carry big bags and take children to the toilet, all of which calls for differently designed toilets for them. Yet the design of public toilets does nothing to acknowledge this difference. Moreover, whereas men's urinals are open through the night, most women's toilets close at 9pm, sending the clear message that women are not expected to – and not supposed to – be out in public at night.

The provision of infrastructure such as transport and toilets does not necessarily mean women will be safe from rape/assault in public, but it does enshrine women's right to be there, and in doing so perhaps contribute to a reduction in victim blaming, arguably performing the opposite function to that of those closed toilets. Infrastructure does not change attitudes but it does make a difference. The gang rape and murder of the young woman in Delhi in December 2012 was facilitated in part by the lack of adequate public transport, which meant that she was travelling in a private bus. Public transport, especially buses, has many checks and balances, which means that it is much less likely that such crimes will occur there.

Urban designers and planners have repeatedly pointed out that the way to make a public space safer is not by keeping out those perceived to be "undesirables" but by encouraging more and more of those considered "desirables". The irony of the matter is that in Mumbai far more energy is spent on keeping people out of public spaces than in inviting them in. To begin with, the quantity of public open spaces in the city is dismal and it is fast receding. Where open public spaces do exist, they often tend to be badly maintained or officiously policed, both of which discourage popular use. Open spaces such as parks are frequently seen as an invitation for what is termed "anti-social activity" and, as a result, controlled through both physical means such as high

In recent years, while women have been present in increasing numbers in higher education and the workforce and even in political office, this has not translated into equal access, much less rights to public space for women

walls and fences and administrative means such as "controlled timings". This anxiety is then reflected in relentless policing of these parks, premised on the exclusion of the majority who might be variously seen to be impoverished, overwhelmingly numerous or visually unappealing. Access fundamentally dependent on surveillance ultimately remains limited. The design of public facilities determined by an exclusionary impulse actually makes these spaces inaccessible and sometimes even unsafe for women.

Parks as open public spaces are also used to impose a specific "moral vision" of order on the city. In Mumbai, as in many →

ABOVE: Women in Mumbai often feel threatened in public streets and squares

→ cities across the country, this morality is peculiarly directed at public displays of romantic affection, and sometimes even the mere presence of couples. In a city where the private home is often a space of crowding, couples seek privacy along the promenades or in parks across the city. In some ways, the public offers them an anonymous sanctuary. But not for too long. Increasingly, in city public spaces, couples are being censured for holding hands, which is construed as threatening the "moral fabric of Indian society". In the present, such moral policing is aimed at heterosexual couples, but this is reflective of the invisibility of same-sex couples rather than any progressive politics. If heterosexual couples find it difficult to find undisturbed spaces, for same-sex couples it is virtually impossible.

Design in urban public spaces is not just important at the micro level of individual parks and toilets but at the macro level of the overall planning of the city. Over the past few years Mumbai has been steadily undergoing a makeover, primarily achieved by segregating spaces for different people and activities.

This tunnel vision of the city is unfriendly to women at multiple levels. Zoning spaces on the basis of use into residential and commercial areas is detrimental to women's mobility. Our research shows that women have more access to public space in mixed-use areas, where shops and business establishments are open late into the night, ensuring activity at all times. Moreover, when public space falls off the agenda in planning, what is left becomes increasingly privatised, policed and often fraught with risk. Contrary to common-sense notions of urban "beautification", clean lines and people-less streets do not equal comfort or safety for women, who often seem to prefer a degree of chaos, ambiguity and multiplicity to univalent notions of cleanliness and order.

Taking risks is only possible, especially for women, when the infrastructure is in place – when the streets are well-illuminated, when the public transport system runs day and night and when safe toilets for women are accessible at all hours. These might not be adequate by themselves, but they are essential conditions for making city public spaces more accessible to women. Such facilities are not luxuries bestowed by the state but the right of all citizens.

When public infrastructure disregards women's particular needs it in effect renders women invisible in the city, de-legitimising their right to be heard in the process of shaping the city. Women's presence in the city – on the streets as opposed to in privatised public spaces like malls – stakes a claim to women's right to participate in the everyday politics of city life. In recent years, while women have been present in increasing numbers in higher education and the workforce and even in political office, this has not translated into equal access, much less rights to public space for women. Women will only have a real political voice when these voices can be heard, not only in the rarefied spaces of the Panchayat, legislative assembly or parliament but also on the streets. Occupying the streets – in purposeful and even in playful, purposeless ways – is not merely a matter of women gaining access to physical public space but also about them laying full claim to citizenship of the city. It is about women finding a visible space in the larger urban discourse and in the public conversations and debates that help shape the city and its politics.

Public space represents what the city might mean for its citizens – the possibilities it creates for them to become part of the city, to belong to it and have it belong to them. When we say "become part of the city" we mean in a visceral sense – where all citizens can go out there and claim the city with their bodies, walking its streets, strolling along its edges, watching its movement and partaking of the thrills of risking pleasure in the city. If we can imagine this we can imagine a radically altered city.

©Shilpa Phadke, Shilpa Ranade and Sameera Khan
www.indexoncensorship.org

Shilpa Phadke, Shilpa Ranade and **Sameera Khan** are co-authors of Why Loiter? Women and Risk on Mumbai Streets, published by Penguin India @whyloiter

Fast Forward

42(3): 46/49 | DOI: 10.1177/0306422013500187

Web access is coming soon to almost everywhere, including the world's most remote communities. **Brian Pellot** finds out from the world's digital development gurus what is about to change, and what difference this will make to people's lives

GOOGLE GURU AND executive chairman Eric Schmidt predicts that everyone (all seven-plus billion of us) will be connected by 2020. Schmidt and his co-author Jared Cohen paint a world of promise in their latest book The New Digital Age, but others have interpreted their vision as naive, undesirable, or impossible.

It's easy to look at current growth rates in internet use and dismiss predictions of ubiquitous access as absurd. But real techno-

What hinders freedom of expression most dramatically is often not censorship but other disadvantages

logical improvements, coupled with shifts in infrastructure, development and behaviour, will undoubtedly change how we express ourselves in the coming years. More communities – long isolated and marginalised by political, geographic and economic constraints – are already communicating in ways that were once thought to be impossible. How will technological shifts in the next five years continue to enhance freedom of expression?

Leila Janah is founder and CEO of Samasource, a non-profit business that gives

digital work in the form of microtasks to thousands of disadvantaged young people and women around the world. She says: "What hinders freedom of expression most dramatically is often not censorship but other disadvantages. The internet, however, has started to level this playing field – every piece of hardware with a wi-fi connection is a tool with which anyone can teach and learn, dream and plan, seek workers and get hired."

A fundamental shift around technological development patterns is already shaping how local communities interact. Ken Banks, who founded kiwanja.net and Frontline SMS, and who has worked in mobile development for more than a decade, predicts that Western NGOs will soon no longer dominate the information and communication technologies for development (ICT4D) sector. Banks says communities will play a greater role in developing tech solutions to problems as more local organisations and digital aficionados learn to program.

Ushahidi's mobile internet modem BRCK, currently under developzment, is a good example of local innovation expanding access to communications in Africa and beyond. This modem doesn't need a constant power source, so it works better in countries with unreliable supplies. Kenya-based Ushahidi is already well known for its open-source mapping software used to monitor elections and crises around the world. Ushahidi plans to ship the first lot of BRCKs in November 2013 to its Kickstarter backers who helped fund its development (read Ushahidi's Heather Bond in Index on Censorship's December 2012 issue, http://ioc.sagepub.com/).

Despite growth in the number of local companies like Ushahidi, some argue that "digital colonialism" is likely to control ICT infrastructure in many developing societies for the foreseeable future. As Cecil Rhodes connected Africa with railway tracks in the late 19th century, Chinese companies are now laying fibre-optic cables and competing for telecom contracts to serve the continent's billion inhabitants. Some of the big US companies are also working to spread internet access to once unreachable communities.

But certainly some of the current innovations are really starting to take off. Project Loon is a new Google initiative that uses solar-powered balloons to deliver internet access to the world's remotest regions. The balloons create a new network which people in remote locations can connect to using a special antenna. Google started testing the project in June with several balloons in rural New Zealand. Resembling giant jellyfish, the balloons fully inflate as air pressure drops and they approach 18,200 metres above sea level. If successful, Project Loon aims to bring fast and affordable internet to areas well beyond the reach of traditional cables.

An already successful initiative but one that still holds great promise for connecting more communities in the coming years is the Worldwide Interoperability for Microwave Access. This wireless communications standard, sometimes called "wi-fi on steroids", is used to cheaply bring broadband access to remote locations and developing cities. WiMAX networks have expanded rapidly across Asia and elsewhere in recent years and are expected to reach one billion users by the end of this year, and many more by 2020.

ABOVE: Innovations should bring connections to remote parts of Africa, and bring additional facilities as railways did in the 19th century.

Many new advances in mobile and online computing have the potential to create jobs for those in poverty

Aleph Molinari, founder of the Mexico-based non-profit Fundación Proaccesso, is optimistic about technology's role in advancing free expression but worries that governments will hijack innovations, using mass surveillance and censorship in the name of national security to suppress dissent. "When used appropriately, technology can be used to build relationships in com- →

ABOVE: Google Loon balloons will help web access take off

→ munities, foster positive communication, and politically empower people," he says. Janah agrees with Molinari but says there is still a long way to go. "Many new advances in mobile and online computing have the potential to create jobs for those in poverty – they simply aren't yet being used to do so."

Education for all

Beyond technology and infrastructure, shifts in online education will continue to improve freedom of expression. Massive open online courses (MOOCs) like Coursera, Udacity and edX are already attracting millions of students from all corners of the globe, eager to learn hundreds of subjects. Clarissa

Shen, vice-president of Strategic Business and Marketing at Udacity, says that more collaboration between MOOCs, NGOs, governments, universities, and industry leaders will be necessary to make education accessible and affordable for everyone. As these free and inexpensive classes expand, and more people find reliable internet access at home, in cyber cafés or on mobiles, the digital divide and its implications for literacy, income and opportunity is expected to shrink.

The United Nations argues that high-speed internet is necessary for achieving development goals, and its special rapporteur on freedom of expression has described internet access as a right. As digital technologies improve and expand, new voices will inevitably come online. But increased internet access will not necessarily enhance freedom of expression. As the Edward Snowden leaks made clear and as Molinari warns, states and corporations can use our online communications against individuals. The same Chinese companies setting up Africa's infrastructure are also competing to sell security and surveillance expertise to regional governments. New and old internet users alike are being warned to be wary of how rapid changes in technology affect fundamental rights to freedom of expression and privacy.

In the coming years, the quality of digital access in terms of openness, speed, neutrality and freedom from surveillance and censorship should be considered as critical a concern as the ubiquity of access. The digital divide cannot be bridged if repressive state and corporate policies produce chilling effects and restrict the willingness or ability of individuals to express themselves freely.

At a Google event on free speech earlier this year, Schmidt described how technological innovations are enhancing voices and opening new spaces for dissent. Ensuring that dissent outweighs the repression that can follow will be one of the greatest challenges facing digital freedom of expression through 2020 and beyond. ☒

©Brian Pellot
www.indexoncensorship.org

HORIZON SPOTTING: Five digital developments expected to enhance free speech

1) WiMAX: Affordable Worldwide Interoperability for Microwave Access networks are expected to reach one billion users by the end of this year, and many more by 2020

2) MOOCs: Massive Open Online Courses will deliver high quality interactive education to millions more people in the coming years

3) BRCK: Durable mobile internet modems will keep people online when traditional internet connections and electricity fail

4) Cheap smartphones: The sub-US$100 smartphone made internet access affordable for millions. But as technology improves and production costs drop, a sub-$50 smartphone could expand internet access to millions more

5) Project Loon: Innovative private ventures like Google's Project Loon are likely to deliver affordable internet access to the world's remotest regions

Brian Pellot is director of global strategy and religious freedom editor at Religion News Service. Prior to this, he was digital policy adviser for Index. He tweets @brianpellot

Credit: Murad Sezer/Reuters

ABOVE: Police use teargas and water cannons to disperse protesters in Taksim Square, Istanbul, 6 July 2013

Click to hear #citizenvoices?

42(3): 50/54 | DOI: 10.1177/0306422013501772

Political movements which once fought for freedom and prosperity are now trying to close down debate in the name of stabilising new democracies, while internet restrictions stymie people's power to fight back, says **Dhananjayan Sriskandarajah**

WE LIVE IN a time of momentous change, particularly when it comes to communications. The internet and mobile revolutions hold great promise for people to connect with each other, not just to socialise but also to mobilise. They create unprecedented opportunities to hold governments to account by opening up official data and popular monitoring of service delivery (imagine Tripadvisor for public services), and facilitating forms of direct democracy that would have been unimaginable even a couple of decades ago.

The numbers behind the trends are staggering. Any day now there will be more active mobile phones on the planet than there are people; two billion of us already have mobile broadband subscriptions. Global internet traffic is growing at a compound annual growth rate of 23 per cent, and there are already billions of devices connected to the internet gathering and generating vast amounts of data.

All this holds huge potential for citizens. Way back in 2001, we saw text messages helping to mobilise mass protests against the president of the Philippines (who called →

→ his ousting the "coup de text"). In 2007, ushahidi.org helped citizens monitor election violence in Kenya and, more recently, there was the amazing use of the internet and social media during the Arab Spring protests.

Yet amidst this euphoria there are signs that, despite having ever-increasing access to the tools to have their voices heard, there are still millions around the world who are not being heard or whose voice simply doesn't count. Indeed, the gap between the potential for amplified citizen voice and the reality of large numbers of marginalised voices seems to be increasing.

while solidarity and unity are crucial during liberation struggles, debate and dissent are vital to promote both vibrant democracies and economic prosperity

We know that in the developed world, new technologies and social media have not necessarily broadened participation, with a vocal minority dominating communication channels. If we look across the rest of the world, there are serious threats to citizen participation – from poverty, and from repressive regimes, to cynical ways in which emancipatory technologies are being used against activists. We have a long way to go before we truly liberate citizens' voices around the world.

Barriers to being heard

Globally, the greatest barrier to citizen participation remains poverty. Around half the world's population lives on less than US$2.50 a day and one in four of us on this planet does not have access to electricity. The fact that there are more mobile phones than flushing toilets around the world may be a reminder of how prevalent new technologies have become but also a reminder that the lack of some basic old technologies severely limits the ability of many people to live full lives and exercise active citizenship.

The gap in connectivity is also palpable. Some three-quarters of people in the developed world have mobile internet connections, allowing them to access unfathomable amounts of information and connect with unfathomable numbers of people instantly. Yet only 10 per cent of Africans enjoy such access.

Worst of all, the voices of the poor do not even feature where they ought to. For example, in recent discussions about what will replace the Millennium Development Goals (MDGs) when they "expire" at the end of 2015, there were numerous public consultations – many held in the nicest hotels in the most exotic locations – but there were few opportunities for the people who are supposed to be the beneficiaries of such "development" to shape priorities. Examples such as the Participate Initiative (an attempt to collate the lessons of participatory exercises involving the poor) and My World 2015 (a large-scale survey) are rare examples of gathering citizens' voices to inform and influence global decision-making.

In many parts of the world, even where people have the necessary means and tools, the space in which citizens can speak up or mobilise is being threatened.

The situation in many African countries is particularly acute, especially where political movements that once fought for freedom and prosperity, having assumed power, are now trying to clamp down on civic space. What they ignore at their peril is that, while solidarity and unity are crucial during liberation struggles, debate and dissent are vital to promote both vibrant democracies and economic prosperity.

Across the continent, we are told that "young democracies" or countries with a "fragile peace" could easily be destabilised if the government were to loosen its grip on civic space. In Zimbabwe, the activities of local civil society organisations are attacked because they are allegedly plotting regime change on behalf of foreign governments. In Kenya, Tanzania and Uganda the state has the power to de-register a civil society organisation without reason and without the intermediation of a court of law. In Ethiopia, groups that receive more than 10 per cent of funding from foreign sources cannot undertake advocacy or human rights work.

The potential of arguably the most liberating tool for citizen voice – the internet – is also under threat from new restrictions that clamp down on the ability of citizens to mobilise or hold governments to account. Not only do citizens of many countries face some kind of restriction on their online freedoms, but in some countries governments are leaving internet access open but are monitoring activity and dissent. They allow online freedom of expression but use the evidence – often gathered through online surveillance – to round up, jail and sometimes attack people who dare to disagree.

Protest and participation

Another area of concern is how governments react to popular protests. In many countries around the world, governments are failing one of the fundamental tests of a working democracy, namely how they respond to protests. In Cambodia, land rights activists opposing official plans to forcibly acquire land for big companies have been subjected to brutal attacks by security forces and lengthy prison terms. In Honduras, peasant farmer groups involved in land disputes with companies have been subjected to murderous attacks. In India, peaceful activists ideologically opposed to the government's economic policy have been charged, under draconian laws, of being members of outlawed terrorist organisations. In Canada, non-profit groups opposed to the conservative government's policy of loosening environmental restrictions to enable extraction of oil and gas from ecologically sensitive zones

have been subjected to surveillance and funding cuts while being accused of obstructing the country's economic development.

In some cases, the rhetoric about protests is just as worrying as what actually happens to the protestors. The Turkish Prime Minister's dismissal of mass protests in Taksim Square in June 2013 as being led by a handful of looters and vandals, manipulated

In Cambodia, land rights activists opposing official plans to forcibly acquire land for big companies have been subjected to brutal attacks by security forces and lengthy prison terms

by foreign forces, is typical of how leaders refuse to treat citizens' grievances with the respect they deserve. Western leaders have similarly dismissed the Occupy movement and *indignados* as fringe elements without clear vision or majority support.

Here lies the challenge for those of us interested in promoting citizen voice around the world. We live in an era where it is easier and cheaper than ever before to communicate; yet it is also an era in which the barriers

We are at the cusp of a new era of citizen participation

to equal participation are as significant as ever. In some cases it is poverty that prevents people from having the wherewithal to be full members of the polity, in others it is the attacks on the space in which people can mobilise, and in yet others, where protests can and do happen, it is the lack of constructive response from those in power. It is little wonder then that when I talk to civil society leaders around the world that so many of them are pessimistic about the future. →

→ I remain optimistic that we are at the cusp of a new era of citizen participation. History teaches us that it is futile for governments to curb people's freedoms. It is a question of when, not if, citizens rise up to challenge and often overthrow political systems in which their rights are curtailed. New technologies are making it easier to access information, connect with other like-minded people, and mobilise large numbers of people. Over time, the use of these technologies will close the gap between the potential for magnifying citizen's voices, including marginalised groups, and today's reality of listening to the loud few. These technologies will provide innovative ways for citizens to make their voices heard and to hold those in power to account. It may not be instant, but communications technology will continue to help revolutionise citizen action and amplify citizen voices. In the end, people power will prevail. ☒

©Dhananjayan Sriskandarajah
www.indexoncensorship.org

Dr **Dhananjayan Sriskandarajah** is Secretary General of CIVICUS, the World Alliance for Citizen Participation. www.civicus.org; @civicusSG

THE TIMES
CHELTENHAM FESTIVALS

LITERATURE 13

in association with
Waterstones

THE TIMES CHELTENHAM LITERATURE FESTIVAL

TICKETS ON SALE NOW

4–13 OCT 2013

CLASSICS
POLITICS & CURRENT AFFAIRS
Comedy
FICTION
LIFESTYLE

POETRY
HISTORY
STUDIO STAGE AND SCREEN

BOX OFFICE 0844 880 8094

f 🐦 📷 📌 **#cheltlitfest**

cheltenhamfestivals.com

Registered Charity No.251765

The sound of silence

42(3): 56/61 | DOI: 10.1177/0306422013501776

As the United Nations opens with a tribute to Malian musicians this month, documentary maker **Johanna Schwartz** asks if after the recent election musicians, persecuted by Islamists under the former regime, are coming back to the country

MALI IS THE only country in the world to have a special class in society reserved for musicians – they are known as the *griots*. *Griots* are given the responsibility of communicating the oral history of the tribe or village, as well as entertaining with song and stories. And unlike other developing or middle-income nations, women and men are equally revered. These musicians have passed their lyrical storytelling on to their sons and daughters for generations. They are the lifeblood of Malian society. But that changed on 22 August 2012 – the day that Osama Ould Abdel Kader, a spokesperson for MUJAO, the Movement for Oneness and Jihad in West Africa, proclaimed that music was forbidden.

Members of MUJAO and a loose association of other extremist groups attacked mosques, libraries and mobile phone towers. By July 2012, as many as half of Timbuktu's ancient shrines were destroyed. In addition, there were attacks on Mali's most powerful cultural and political commentators – the *griots*.

Before this summer's elections, musicians had their instruments and equipment smashed, radio stations were torched and even young people with musical-sounding ringtones on their mobile phones were beaten. At the same time those accused of

"We don't have a free press, instead we have musicians"

....

In Mali, music is the people's source of information. Music is the press; it is the news. In Mali we don't have a free press, instead it is the musicians who pass on information and tell the stories of our history, says Fadimata Walet Oumar

I became a musician after being involved with humanitarian work and living abroad. I was contacted by a festival who wanted an all-female Tuareg band to perform and at this time there was no such thing. They asked if we could form a band and I said of course, nothing is impossible – it could be hard but we can try. And so we did. I found performing at the festival very liberating, as we were able to share our story with so many different people. As musicians, we could tell the entire world about our culture, our lives and the problems of our people. Music is a miracle, it is an important part of

adultery were being stoned to death, and there were public whippings for failing to wear the veil. Many Malians had fled over the borders, creating the largest mass migration the southern Sahara has ever seen. Those who stayed were shocked into submission, complying with strict sharia principles.

Mali's cultural class were on the run, fleeing to refugee camps in Mauritania or Burkina Faso and, for those who had European record labels, to Paris. Fatoumata Diawara, a relative newcomer to the Mali music scene, immediately began to organise her fellow musicians from her base in Paris. The result was the Voices United for Mali, a super group of more than 40 singers and musicians. Their single, "Mali-Ko", urges all Malians to stand up for peace in the wake of the extremist occupation.

The lyrics argue:

The world adored our country, so why now are we tearing each other apart before their very eyes?

Our Mali will never belong to those people. This great nation will not be their victim.

Listen to me: we must take care now or our children will never know the real story of our country.

As cultural freedom suffered, so did journalistic freedom. Reporters Sans Frontières Press Freedom Index 2013 showed that Mali suffered the biggest annual fall in freedom of the press of any country in the past year.

In the capital, Bamako, Mali's temporary president Dioncounda Traoré, in place after a bungled coup attempt earlier in the year, tried to combat these groups with an untrained and even more undisciplined

Music teaches you how to live, how society can grow and change. The world without music is impossible to imagine

army. In just a few short months, Mali was out of control.

How did this all begin? And how did the freedom of Mali's citizens disappear almost overnight?

Travelling into Mali from Algeria in the north, opportunistic extremists from MUJAO and AQUIM (al Qaeda in the Islamic Maghreb) joined forces with the MNLA (National Movement for the Liberation of Azawad), a group of northern Tuareg separatists. The extremists quickly turned the →

how a civilisation develops. Music teaches you how to live, how society can grow and change. The world without music is impossible to imagine.

Before the Islamists had even reached Timbuktu, I had left Mali and gone to a refugee camp in Burkina Faso. I somehow knew this was going to be a dark time for Mali – especially for its musicians. My band ended up being split between Mauritania and Burkina Faso, because when we chose to flee we headed for the closest border. At that time, some of the band were closer to Mauritania and I was closer to Burkina Faso. I went to the camp on 2 February 2012 and whilst I knew the situation was very bad, I could never have imagined just how cruel and dark the conflict would become. I could never in my life imagine that they would ban music. I could not think it – I did not believe it was even possible. It happened so fast, and I truly believed that life as we knew it in Mali was over. All the information and news is passed on to the people through music. These groups wanted to stop the people from being given information and they wanted to stop us telling our →

ABOVE: Musician Fadimata "Disco" Walet Oumar fled Mali as the extremists took power

For Malians, and especially its musicians, this meant that their way of life was over, and their ancient culture was in the process of being destroyed forever. By January 2013, a year after the start of the conflict, the French and ECOWAS armies had arrived and the uprising and invasion had escalated into a fully-fledged war. However, now, with attention from around the world focused on the struggle, there are some signs that musicians in Mali can start to feel a little more confident.

Malian musician Fadimata "Disco" Walet Oumar was one of those who fled at the start of the conflict. "I could never in my life imagine that they would ban music. I could not think it. I did not believe it was even possible. It happened so fast, and I truly believed that life as we knew it in Mali was over."

Also featured on the "Mali-Ko" peace single is Bassekou Kouyate, a Jimi Hendrix-style master of the *ngoni*, an ancient traditional lute found throughout West Africa. Bassekou has worked with international superstars such as Nitin Sawhney and Arcade Fire. On the day fighting broke out in Bamako he was in the recording studio with his band, which is comprised of his wife, sons and brother.

He says: "The day of the coup I got to the studio around noon and began working on my new album. Around four we

→ fight from a movement for Tuareg separatism into a battle for the establishment of a full-blown fundamentalist state.

After just a few short months, the bold and public-facing Salafist takeover was complete and the Tuareg cause completely sidelined. The New Yorker described it thus: "For decades, al Qaeda had acted as a largely rootless and amorphous agent of terror. Now its brash new affiliate had secured itself a state."

→ history to the next generation.

Life without music is not possible, and for me personally I would rather die than never be able to perform, create or listen to music again in my life.

At the refugee camp we continued to play music, organising dances and parties. One of the important things about music is that it allows you to forget, to put your problems out of your mind for a little while. But sometimes I would get so upset, seeing more and more people arrive at the refugee camp every day, and hearing the news from Mali, that I would lose my voice, my throat would just close up.

I had to be careful to cover my face and not be identified whilst I was performing as I am well known in Mali – my father and other members of my family are still living in the north and I was very afraid for them. I did not want them to be punished in retaliation for my music.

These events are like the end of the world. These men [who imposed sharia law] are not good, they come from a very bad place. Our culture and our music cannot be separated.

Music plays an important role in the lives of Tuareg women. Our music gives women lib-

started to hear very loud gunfire – 'boom, boom, boom, boom' – and I said: 'What's going on?"' We went outside the studio and there were armed soldiers everywhere. They said they were carrying out a coup d'état because the army wasn't happy because the president wanted to negotiate with the Tuareg [separatists].

"I closed the door. I was so angry. And then I said: "I'm not going to let this get to me. We're here to make music." There were lots of foreigners here who had come because of my new album – Germans, English people and others – and then suddenly Mali was under lockdown. It's all down to the Islamists – they caused all these problems in Mali." Before the start of the conflict, music was everywhere in Mali. At weddings, nightclubs and feasts, impromptu sessions on street corners, nomad camps in the desert, and the courtyard gardens of the *griots*."

"In Mali it is the music that is the people's source of information, music is the press, it is the news. In Mali we don't have a free press and instead it is the musicians who pass on information and tell the stories of our history. All the information and news is passed on to the people through music," says Fadimata "Disco" Walet Oumar.

At the centre of Mali's music culture in recent years has been the famous Festival in the Desert. For 12 years, it brought some of the world's top musicians to the desert outside of Timbuktu. Though small groups of musicians have been meeting in the desert for centuries, the Festival in the Desert was officially founded in 1991 to create a cultural, and curative, bridge between the northern Tuareg musicians and those in the south. Over the years it has attracted a huge amount of press attention, as well as stars such as Bono and Robert Plant.

Musicians are beginning to trickle back into Mali, and the state of emergency has officially been lifted

Manny Ansar, director of the Festival in the Desert, was born near Timbuktu into a nomadic Tuareg family. Before joining the group that began the Festival in the Desert, he worked in the humanitarian aid field. He remembers the decision to cancel 2013's festival was a necessity, as Timbuktu was one of the three cities where the fighting was the most intense.

But six months later, those battles were won by the Malian armies, in large part →

---

erty. Traditionally women play our music, and that gives us power and rights. We have an important role to play in society and it is through music that we can be heard. These men were seeking to prevent women from participating in their traditional roles. Free-dom of expression is the most important thing in the world, and music is a part of freedom. If we don't have freedom of expression, how can you genuinely have music? ⊠

©Fadimata Walet Oumar
www.indexoncensorship.
org

Fadimata "Disco" Walet Oumar *is the founder and lead singer of Tartit, which consists of five women and four men. Through their music, Tartit seek to preserve a culture currently under attack and have become the world's most famous ambassadors of traditional Tuareg music.*

Disco's organisation promoting women's rights has now been recognised by the United Nations. Tartit, which means union, are all Tuareg from the Kel Antessar tribe who have held sway in the deserts around the historic city of Timbuktu for centuries. They are currently refugees in Burkina Faso

ABOVE: Bassekou Kouyate performs a *ngoni* solo during the Womad Festival

Credit: Soody Ahmad/EMPICS Entertainment

→ **Musicians had their instruments and equipment smashed, radio stations were torched and even young people with musical- sounding ringtones on their mobile phones were beaten**

due to the expertise of the 4,000 French soldiers who intervened in January 2013, after a plea from Mali's government. And although small numbers of the 374,000 displaced people are beginning to return home, many believe that the mujahedeen are in hiding, biding their time, plotting their next moves.

Manny has to decide whether it is safe enough for the 2014 show to go on or not. Should they return to their desert home outside of Timbuktu, or move the festival to Bamako where security can be controlled? Will things have calmed down enough by the beginning of 2014 or will it be 2015, or even later? Many see the festival returning as a benchmark for "things returning to normal" and are eager to show the world that Mali has been restored.

Meanwhile, Manny, as well as many of Mali's more successful artists, are working to keep the music scene together by staging awareness-raising concerts around the world, including the Fuji Rock Festival in Japan, a Festival of the Desert in exile, and a concert at the opening of the United Nations General Assembly in September 2013.

"People have grown desperate and weary of talks of amicable solutions to the crisis one day, armed intervention and UN resolutions the day after, then back to prospects of peaceful negotiations a short while later. Above these frustrations, we are gathering our artists and fans to sing for peace and demonstrate that in Mali not everybody is at war. The brutal sound of weapons and the cries of intolerance are not able to silence the singing of the *griots*," Ansar told Ceasefire magazine.

Historically, armed Islamist groups in Africa do not tend to disappear as quickly as they emerge. Many saw this summer's elections as a benchmark to restore faith in Mali and its government. After the result of the second election in August was declared new president Ibrahim Boubacar Keita told news channels the way the elections were carried out, without significant problems, were a symbol of the new Mali. The nation's citizens are now waiting to see what that new era will bring. Though musicians are beginning to trickle back into Mali now, and the state of emergency has officially been lifted, there is a fear that the freedoms may not be so easily restored and that Mali's musical culture has seen its golden age come and go.

Despite this, the keepers of Mali's history and wisdom, the musicians, refuse to give up. On stage with his family at the Glastonbury Festival in June 2013, Bassekou Kouyate took a break to entreat the enthusiastic crowd in broken English:

"I am very happy now. There is no sharia in Mali, okay? Sharia is finished. It's all done, Mali is good. You all should come to Mali, okay? Mali is the best place in Africa!"

And with that, the band burst into "Ne Me Fatigue Pas", a song they wrote in the midst of the coup attempt. The title translates as "Don't Wear Me Down". ☒

©Johanna Schwartz
www.indexoncensorship.org

Johanna Schwartz is an award-winning documentary filmmaker. Working across the world, with a particular focus on Africa, she has produced and directed films for the BBC, Channel 4, Channel 5, Discovery, National Geographic, the History channel, PBS, CNBC, CNN and MTV, among others. She is currently directing a feature-length film on Mali's conflict and its impact on musicians

ABOVE: Volunteers learn how to use the news platform at Swara

India calling

42(3): 62/67 | DOI: 10.1177/0306422013503065

It's citizen journalism with a twist. Shubhranshu Choudhary and his team have harnessed some simple technology to bring news reporting to a whole region of people in central India who felt abandoned by the traditional media, finds **Rachael Jolley.** Photos by **Purushottam Thakur**

WHEN THE WORLD needs innovation it often looks for the discovery of some cutting-edge technology to solve the problem. But sometimes something simple can provide the answer.

The combination of mobile, internet and radio can really create a democracy in this country

In central India, a journalist who wanted to change the lives of millions of people found his technical challenge solved by a simple, non-smart mobile phone.

Former BBC South Asia producer Shubhranshu Choudhary didn't have to ask the techies to pull something clever out of the box; instead, he needed a bit of technology to which millions of poor people already had access, and once he realised that, he knew where to look. He created a new kind of media service where anyone could call in and leave a message in their own language and suggest or tell a news story; alternatively, →

ABOVE: Women phone in to hear the news

→ they could call and listen to stories left by others.

Many poor, rural people who live in Chhattisgarh and in the forested areas of central India do not speak Hindi or English, the main languages of the Indian media; they don't have access to newspapers or internet news; they live in remote villages, often without running water and schools. They also live at the centre of a region that the Indian government has been pouring troops into for years to tackle the "Maoist insurgency".

For these people, this invention, a media platform called CGNet Swara, was a way of both telling news stories and listening to news from others, using a piece of equipment they either already owned or could get access to.

The latest Indian census (2011) reported that more people had a mobile phone than had inside toilets, with 53 per cent of households in the country owning a mobile phone, compared with only 3.1 per cent having internet access. Take into account the fact that, in addition to these 53 per cent of households, people share mobile phones with others beyond the household, and others use landlines, giving an even wider group access to telephone communication. In fact the Indian telecommunications regulator

TRAI suggest that access to mobile phones stand at around 70 per cent, with this figure at 40 per cent in rural communities.

Choudhary, a Knight International Journalism Fellow, was inspired to create a news platform for this region during his time working for the BBC: "I was travelling from one war zone to another, then wars started near my home. I grew up in central India and I also covered the region for the BBC. When something happens nearer to you, nearer to your heart, it makes you think more. The difference in this case was that I grew up in that area, and the backbenchers in my school – they were the 'terrorists' that the prime minister called the 'biggest internal security threat', and it unnerved me. These were the students that never raised their voices, and how come 25 years later they had become 'terrorists'?"

So he took some time living in the forests of central India with these communities, who were being referred to as Maoists. And he was told by the local people that the system of communicating news, and communicating what was wrong in their lives, was not working for them. "This is a huge community, around 100 million people, and this is a breakdown of communication. Our communication system is still very aristocratic, where a small number of people sitting on top have too much power and the huge majority of people don't have any voice or have very little power to decide what is not heard and what should be heard. When you sit in a village in a small group of people under a tree and discuss the issues, then that discussion is democratic because the medium they use is air, which is not owned by anyone." Democracy or equality disappears when certain people own the medium that transmits the news, he argues, and when a group's voice is not being heard, grudges accumulate. He argues that the absence of those debates leads to dissatisfaction and leaves communities susceptible to groups who come to the forest claiming that they can create something better: "We call it the Maoist problem, but the number of people in the forest who are Maoist is 2 per cent or 5 per cent. They have simple problems such as water, roads, hospitals, jobs, and we didn't deliver because we didn't hear them."

Many people are *adivasis*, marginalised indigenous people, who often have low levels of literacy but have an oral history tradition of passing on news and traditions. "We go to these villages and ask who speaks Hindi without realising that is the language of the rich; 70 to 90 per cent of these people don't speak any language but their mother tongue," said Choudhary.

The huge majority of people don't have any voice or have very little power to decide what is not heard

But users of the new type of news platform introduced by Choudhary don't need to speak another language – they can dial in and leave an audio message of the story they would like to tell in their own language. Areas are broken up into groups, so local people hear from other local people, and there are hundreds of these audio communities. Most of these groups primarily listen to local stories, but occasionally the moderators for the service find a story that they think other groups would be interested in, about a wider issue, and it is shared.

It is a bottom-up model, with communities electing their own moderators who are trained by CGNet on skills such as fact checking and phoning back "reporters" to check up on stories. CGNet also translates stories into Hindi and English and publishes them on its website so a wider group of people can read the stories, as well as providing audio in the original language of the contributor. They get around 500 calls →

ABOVE: Staff work closely with volunteers at the news channel.

DID YOU KNOW ?

104 million households in India have radios, double the number that have TVs

53 per cent of homes have mobile phones, but only 47 per cent have an indoor toilet

India Census, 2011

→ per day, 50 of which they record. After checks, about five recordings are broadcast.

"We have a strict cross check and filtering process, including calling back to encourage them, and if it is opinion it needs to be clearly labelled," said Choudhary. He points out that the difference between this system and the traditional newspaper editor is that these moderators are elected by the community, and so actually represent them.

Stories are varied and range from one report that a forest ranger asked for bribes totalling RR99,000 rupees (US$1,628), to another about school dinners not arriving, while a third reports on high numbers of blind and mentally ill children in an *advasi*

village. Swara is clearly having impact too: days after the report about the numbers of blind village children, a health team arrived to find out more, and the ranger has now repaid his bribes.

CGNet is carrying out a wide range of activities to enhance the smooth running of the news platform, including training young people as translators and training adults as moderators, but it is hoped that training will be devolved to the community in the longer term. It is working towards what it calls a "temple model", in which people train each other: a sort of trickle-down technique for learning. It is also publishing all its learning and knowledge about its technology so other groups can set up similar projects in other regions.

The next step is shortwave radio, which would allow them to reach much bigger audiences still, including those who cannot read. There are obstacles though. Currently there is a news radio reporting monopoly held by the government-backed national All India Radio, although there have been some suggestions that this regulation may be relaxed. So to push onwards CGNet is looking to work with an international provider such as the BBC, with whom Chaudhary has held initial conversations.

"The combination of mobile, internet and radio can really create a democracy in this country. If you can link with radio you have to do so from outside the country because India doesn't allow shortwave radio. If we want to do shortwave linkage we can only do it from outside India."

Around 104 million Indian households have access to a radio, double the number with televisions, making radio an extremely powerful communication tool.

Right now, Chaudhary is looking for a partner to help make that next step happen, but he is confident that this type of news service is making a difference.

"It is not solving all problems, but you can create some hope, you can combat some problems. You can tackle the attitude of hopelessness." ☒

©Rachael Jolley
www.indexoncensorship.org

Rachael Jolley is the editor of Index on Censorship magazine

③ IMAGINE, YOU MARRY A **MARQUIS**. IN A MARQUEE! YOU'RE **MANIFESTLY MAGNIFICENT!** AND YET YOU END UP **MARTYRED** BY **MARGINALISATION!** WHAT MERETRICIOUS MASQUE OF **MAYHEM** & **MEDIOCRITY** HAS **MARKED** YOU DOWN FOR **MAULING?** ARE YOU **TRULY** THE **MARMITE** OF MANKIND? ARE YOU **REALLY** SO MANKY YOU MERIT **MARGINALISATION?** WERE YOU BORN IN A **MANGER**, OR WITH A **MINGE?** ARE YOU **MANGLED**, **MANNERED** OR MERELY **MAD?** DO YOU LOOK MORE LIKE A **MANATEE** THAN A MODEL FROM **MANHATTAN?** OR IS IT MONEY— **MOOLAH**— THE **MARKET**— THAT'S **MUCKED YOU UP?** WE'LL FIND OUT!

④ BUT FIRST— THIS MESSAGE FROM OUR **CORPORATE SPONSOR**

EEK!

⑤ Shortly...

WELCOME BACK, AND... HEY! WHERE'S SHE GONE?

I'M OVER HERE! IN THE MARGIN!

13

Global view *by* **Kirsty Hughes**

42(3): 70/71 | DOI: 10.1177/0306422013502136

PRIVACY AND DIGITAL freedom were key topics of debate in Germany's general election campaign. And the same issues are set to dominate a big chunk of European and international political debate through the autumn when the European Union's leaders will be discussing a range of digital issues, from competitiveness to privacy to free expression online.

And, in parallel, various major international summits loom – on digital freedom, internet governance and cybersecurity. The ambitious EU-US talks on a transatlantic free trade area are already getting tangled up in these debates too.

Opposition politicians have labelled Angela Merkel and her allies too weak in their response to the US

But will all this summitry, negotiations and political debate benefit digital freedom of expression? And in the wake of the Edward Snowden revelations about major US and UK mass surveillance and snooping programmes, as well as leaks and allegations about similar programmes in France, Sweden and Germany too, can Europe lead on digital freedom any more?

As these crucial political debates unfold in the months ahead, we may start to see the answers to these questions.

It was Snowden's revelations of US mass surveillance that brought privacy and digital freedom to the heart of Germany's election campaign. With memories still fresh of Stasi monitoring of the East German population, the debate in Germany has been fierce. Opposition politicians have labelled Angela Merkel and her allies too weak in their response to the US, and the German media has persistently questioned how much government and secret services already knew on the US and UK's mass surveillance. Merkel has demanded rapid EU action on new data protection laws – and called on President Obama to respect the privacy rights of German citizens.

But even in the face of such massive international surveillance, EU member states are not likely to rupture relationships with their key ally the US. And sure enough, ambitious transatlantic trade talks started on schedule in July – with a sweetener from the US offering EU-US working groups to discuss the secret surveillance. How much ordinary citizens will learn about such transatlantic talks between spooks remains to be seen.

The EU, the US, and a range of other nations will all turn up at the Seoul Summit on cybersecurity in October 2013 to share worries about how to defend both digital freedom and security in the face of intrusive digital attacks and snooping from hostile states. Ironies abound here: how can the US or UK continue to argue for digital freedom at global internet summits while undertaking a massive international collection of phone, email, internet and other communications data? How can they continue with their attempts to persuade states like Brazil or South Africa to join them in standing up to Russia's and China's attempts to agree top-down international control of the net? And how can they worry about cybersecurity when they seem to have intruded on the electronic communications of most countries around the world?

The same questions will be asked at the next summit rendezvous in Bali, where the annual Internet Governance Forum (IGF) will take place at the end of October. The IGF is seen as the quintessential summit for an open and free internet – the clumsily labelled "multi-stakeholder" approach to net governance. But the term multi-stakeholder means both that civil society and business, as well as governments, turn up, discuss and play a part in a networked way in ensuring the internet flourishes; and it means that the US dominance of key parts of that system continues. In the wake of the mass surveillance revelations, it will be no surprise if India or Brazil, as well as China and Russia, start to question this even more strongly.

In some ways the EU is doing its best. EU leaders are due to agree freedom of expression guidelines – online and off – before the end of the year, and this will be a crucial part of its future dialogues with other countries on human rights. The EU's October summit will look at digital competitiveness – and perhaps privacy too. And the European Parliament has set up a welcome and vital committee of inquiry into the Snowden revelations.

But in this rush of summits and debates, more information is still to emerge. The UK and France have big surveillance programmes too and Sweden has laws that, like the US, permit snooping on "foreign" communications to a greater extent than on domestic ones – there are suggestions that so do other EU states such as Germany and the Netherlands.

True, none of these EU states are rushing towards China's approach to internet censorship – with firewalls, blocks, censorship and harassment. They are still democracies.

But the EU should sort out a tough and common approach that stops mass surveillance and protects privacy and free speech online. If not, it will find that its leverage in the international debate on digital freedom and its influence on countries like India, Brazil, Kenya and many more has disappeared. ☒

©Kirsty Hughes
www.indexoncensorship.org

Kirsty Hughes is CEO at Index on Censorship

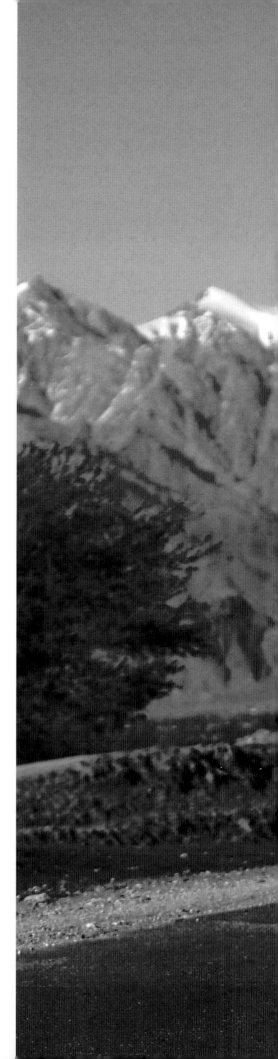

IN FOCUS

In this section

Afghan heartland

42(3): 72/78 | DOI: 10.1177/0306422013502617

Just months before troops pull out, **Charlotte Cross**, who served with the British Army in Helmand, reports on how the army has worked with local women to help change attitudes and radically reform what women can do in their communities

ABOVE: : A woman walks along a road just outside Kabul

ABOVE: Afghan women voting at an election in Gereshk

IWAS SHOCKED WHEN I heard about the murder of Islam Bibi in July 2013. A 37-year-old mother of three living in Helmand, Lieutenant Bibi (to use her hard-earned rank) had joined the Afghan National Police some nine years earlier. I met her back in 2009, when I was in Helmand reporting on the work of the UK Task Force. She told me she wanted to make a difference in her country, she wanted to defeat the Taliban, she wanted to stop them ever coming back into power. She'd suffered threats and intimidation, even from her own family, over what she was doing, but she was determined. There were just seven female police officers

in 2009. Following a recruitment campaign by the British military, today there are more than 30.

Lieutenant Bibi was a trailblazer, a woman who led the way and stood up for what she believed in, on behalf of all the women who don't have a voice. Lieutenant Bibi pushed against the attitudes of conservative relatives and neighbours, in a place where women are usually regarded as second-class citizens. In some of the more remote, rural areas, women are considered lower down the social scale than goats. Goats after all bring in money; women, denied an education and the right to work, do not. But outspoken women in conservative Helmand make certain people angry. She was shot dead, murdered as she left her home in the capital, Lashkar Gah. An extraordinary woman, on an ordinary day, gunned down in broad daylight.

I first arrived in Helmand in August 2006. As an officer in the Territorial Army, I volunteered to deploy for six months to what was then dubbed "the most dangerous place on earth". My job was to try to understand the local population, so I spent much of my time just talking to Afghans. It was five years since the official fall of the Taliban, but I was struck by the fact they were still there, intimidating women from the shadows. At the girls' school in Lashkar Gah, I listened while the headmistress told me the Taliban

Living under the Taliban
....
Banu Khetab

Banu Khetab tells her personal story of life under the Taliban, witnessing attacks on women and trying to make things change

I am an Afghan and lived through the civil war and the Taliban regime. Although I had to leave in late 1998, I was going back and forth to support community development programmes in different provinces of Afghanistan. I then returned in 2001 and stayed until the end

of 2011. I worked as a women's rights activist and development practitioner in civil society and government projects. I also had my own NGO for women empowerment.

It was challenging to be a women's rights activist in Afghanistan. I remember one time in

1998 I was supposed to provide training in office work to women in one of the urban districts of Kabul. A woman from the area informed the Taliban of the plans. On our way, my colleague and I saw a car following us. My 12-year-son was my male escort, which is called *mahram*

had threatened to cut off her fingers if she didn't give up her job.

Fouzia was the head of the women's centre in Lashkar Gah, a small tatty building where women gathered for mutual support. They learnt skills there, like sewing and IT, so they could start small tailoring businesses or find a job. The women would travel to the centre wearing the burka, afraid of being seen. Their fears were not unfounded. Fouzia would hide her handbag beneath the burka's flowing robes, so nobody would recognise her. She'd already been attacked a few months earlier. A man on a motorbike rode up beside her car, emptying his AK47 into her driver.

They were terrified that a female suicide bomber would try to attack their centre. A female military policewoman taught them how to search burka-clad women for explosives or other weapons. We started a project to build them a security wall, and a guard post.

A few years later, I visited Fouzia again. The Provincial Reconstruction Team (civilians who work for the Department for International Development, the UK's Foreign and Commonwealth Office and USAID), known as the PRT and attached to the UK military task force, had built them a brand new women's centre in a safer part of town. Projects were going on all over Helmand, to help women get an education, acquire skills and find work.

A small radio station in the centre of Lashkar Gah now employs a group of female journalists, who disguise themselves on their way to work.

In some of the more remote, rural areas, women are considered lower down the social scale than goats. Goats after all bring in money; women, denied an education and the right to work, do not

Women still face so much resistance, but progress is gaining pace. The Afghan Tailoring Company is female-run, employing 30 skilled and unskilled female workers. They've learnt about marketing, increased their range of clothes, and opened a shopfront to increase passing trade.

In February, a business development programme sent 11 women from Helmand on business planning training in neighbouring Kandahar. And of 14 vocational training programmes across Helmand, five are exclusively for women, teaching →

and I had to have him or my uncle, brother or husband escort me. This was compulsory, based on Taliban rule. I first told my colleague we should go to another location, but then decided to get out of our taxi. I told the driver to go home and that I would send him a message later. I walked a different route, along a narrow street where the Taliban car was not able to follow me. I went to the home of a local woman and told her to send her son to tell the participants that the training would not happen that day but not to mention anything about who we were. At the original location, we would have been surrounded by the Taliban as they had been informed about us by their female spy from the community.

These were days of fears and difficulties. If we had a knock on our door, I was terrified. If a member of the Taliban walked toward us, we would change our direction. I witnessed the Taliban hit women on their heads in the marketplace because they had nail polish on their feet. One of them fell →

voters in a local election in Helmand. They chose four women to serve with the local government, having their say on education, security and job creation. Two women from Helmand also sit in the national parliament in Kabul, representing the specific interests of women.

In Helmand's second largest town, Gereshk, the District Community Council (DCC) was the first in Helmand to include seats for women, and more than a thousand women voted at the 2012 DCC elections. Just a few years ago, it would be unthinkable to have any sort of training for men and women together. However, over the past two years Gereshk has seen several human rights and other trainings well attended by both men and women. The female DCC members say their experience on the council has helped create a space for women to be represented and express their opinion – in public – on a wide variety of topics.

What about education, so despised and suppressed under Taliban rule?

Where the local people say they need and desire a school, the British military has helped where it can, giving building expertise or help with a grant. In 2009, on a cold and rainy winter's day in the small town of Spin Majid, I visited a couple of large tents, packed with children. There were so many children there weren't enough desks, and

ABOVE: Charlotte Cross with women from the Afghan National Police

→   tailoring, embroidery, computing and English. In the last two years, nearly two thousand graduates have been women.

Women are also slowly breaking into politics. In June 2013, the PRT hosted a local election. More than five hundred women turned up, the largest turnout of female

Credit: Charlotte Cross

Teaching in Helmand can be a dangerous occupation. Teachers have been beheaded in front of their class

→   down, and the other crushed her hand on a metal fence while she was running to escape.

In spite of all the challenges, the results and successes interested me most. I believe that if there are supportive spaces for women, they will always find ways to help themselves and

others, and to work in harmony with their brothers. Our organisation brought change by engaging with the Taliban. We had to show them that in order to survive, women needed food, and that in order to buy food, they needed to work. It was only after consultations between

women and the Taliban that 50 factories, which were closed in Mazar in 1999, were reopened, providing work and food for women.

I believe that you can achieve change when you work with people who believe in the philosophy of that process. That's what we did; we

engaged with those who believed in change. We have a Dari proverb that says "*Koh agar Buland ast Sari khud ra darad*", which means "the mountain is high but there is a way to reach it".

We have gained a lot from international support and our people"s

many were sitting cross-legged on the floor. It was market day, so the teacher wasn't there, but an older boy had taken over the class and was teaching reading and writing. The children were transfixed and concentrating hard. They told me they wanted to be engineers, teachers and doctors, and they wanted to rebuild their war-ravaged country. The tents were eventually replaced with a proper school building.

In Musa Qala, to the far north of Helmand, the American Marine Corps took over from the British in 2010. They too were doing what they could for girls' education. In one of the most strictly conservative towns in Helmand, I visited a tiny school of about 20 girls, desperate for an education. Their teacher was an American-Afghan, who grew up in Kabul. She taught the girls whatever she could a few times a week. She told me that what the Taliban had done to her country made her cry.

Building the school is usually the easy bit. Persuading the local government to fund it, supply books, tables and chairs – that is more difficult. Harder still can be finding the teachers, especially female teachers, to work in the face of threats and intimidation. Teaching in Helmand can be a dangerous occupation. Teachers have been beheaded in front of their class. The journey to and from school is hazardous; children and teachers could be attacked at any time. Families who want to educate their daughters often send them to live with relatives in Lashkar Gah, where the schools are safer.

The only education open to girls under Taliban rule was secret classes in people's homes. Now, the government says half of Helmand's schools are open, teaching 30,000 girls. While only a fifth of the teachers are female, of the 340 future teachers enrolled

Every time I go back, I'm struck by how much has changed. Women now have the right to vote, the right to work, and they have many more freedoms than when I first arrived in 2006

in Helmand's training colleges nearly 70 per cent are female.

Progress for women is strongest in the principal towns of Lashkar Gah and Gereshk. In the rural areas, life is much harder. Patrolling across the fields, or through the mud-walled villages, even in the bazaars, you'll very rarely see women out and →

contribution. We women do not want to lose our space in our society; we have already lost our children, our husbands, fathers, brothers, nephews and cousins. But people feel disappointed and hopeless because there is no clear picture of what will happen in Afghanistan. Afghanistan's future development needs continued attention from the international community. If its security is not stable it will allow terrorism to continue, which will create harm in other parts of the world. It is not the people's fault; they have suffered from over 40 years of war and destruction of their homes and their lives. They deserve more than 80 years of support. Destruction is quicker than rebuilding. Pulling out the troops in 2014 should not result in leaving the people of Afghanistan alone. The Afghan people deserve education, stable economic empowerment and democracy. ⊠

Banu Khetab is a pseudonym

→ about. Plenty of small girls, with their ragged, brightly coloured, sparkly clothes, kohl round their eyes and henna in their hair. But older girls and women are hidden behind the high compound walls of their homes.

In some of these challenging areas, girls and boys are taught the national curriculum inside the home, through the Community Based Education programme. Just over 1,000 girls are currently educated in this way.

Helmand is, however, just a small part of Afghanistan. What happens there may not happen in other provinces, and the capital Kabul seems worlds apart. Last year, I visited Kabul's training centre for the Afghan National Army (ANA), which now proudly boasts the all-female "Malalai Company", containing 30 or so women recruits. Some of them have told their families they are there, and are supported; others keep what they're doing hidden in case of reprisals, including beatings.

In command of them is a British female army officer. They take inspiration from her, and she from them. The female ANA are trained separately from the men, and are viewed as something of an oddity. They are held back, destined for administration posts, and find it difficult to voice opinions in such a patriarchal working environment. Nevertheless, like Lieutenant Bibi, these women are trailblazers.

As with so much in Afghanistan, progress is made in small, quiet steps. Often the outside world doesn't even notice. Every time I go back, I'm struck by how much has changed. Women now have the right to vote, the right to work, and they have many more freedoms than when I first arrived in 2006. They are an inspiration to their daughters, who clamour to go to school, aspiring to careers as doctors, teachers, engineers.

I know many Afghan women warily reflect on the gains they've made, and worry about what will happen when NATO pulls out post-2014. Without foreign support and money, will the Taliban and those who share their beliefs sweep back into power, and undo all that's been achieved in the last decade? I cannot answer that. But what I do know is that Afghan women have already achieved change for themselves, against brutal opposition, and it would be difficult for anyone to reverse it now. Their determination should not be underestimated.

Over the years, I've found it hard to report on or write about this subject, because I'm constantly told the British military didn't go into Afghanistan to protect women's rights. I do accept that. But from what I've seen in Helmand, it's a very fine side effect of the British campaign. X

©Charlotte Cross
www.indexoncensorship.org

Charlotte Cross served in Afghanistan as a British army officer @CharlotteBFBS

Battle chief moves on

42(3): 79/82 | DOI: 10.1177/0306422013503617

As he headed for a new continent, and a job at the Hindustan Times, **Rachael Jolley** spoke to Nic Dawes, editor-in-chief at South Africa's Mail and Guardian, about challenges to press freedom, concerns about wider censorship, the worst and best aspects of the media, and how he sees the years ahead

HIS REPUTATION AS an investigative journalist precedes him. Nic Dawes doesn't shy away from taking on tough stories, and giving oxygen to information that would otherwise stay firmly locked in a drawer.

While editor-in-chief of South Africa's Mail and Guardian (M&G), he has spoken out, again and again, against the Protection of State Information Bill and has written about financial scandals involving South Africa's ruling party despite pressure not to do so, and fought against a media appeals tribunal with members appointed by a parliamentary committee.

All this suggests he is not a man who likes to spend time sitting on a sofa with his feet up. So it comes as no surprise to find out that, while most of us might think a relaxing cycle ride would be a 15 km trip around a woody trail, Dawes recently took on a hardcore 910 km bicycle race across the country, and didn't forget to tweet it for his paper.

The last two years have been marked by tough struggles between leading South African journalists and the South African government, for which stamina and the ability to overcome huge obstacles have definitely been in demand. Dawes recognised it has taken a great deal of time to "make sure

the South African press remains as free as it is now".

Stopping government attempts to push through a new media appeals tribunal, with state appointed members, was one of the challenges, and Dawes was one of the leading

> ## It brought public discussion and a broad public engagement, not just in newsrooms and metropolitan salons, but in poor neighbourhoods in remote locations

combatants in a campaign to stop direct political involvement in media adjudication.

"The ANC has broadly accepted the change and have substantially backed away from a media appeal tribunal. There are still voices of that party calling for statutory regulation so that's not completely over, but I think we made a great deal of progress."

The other major struggle was against government plans to introduce the Protection of State Information Bill, the so-called secrecy bill, which would have made it almost →

ABOVE: A demonstrator protests against the Protection of Information Bill in Cape Town

→ impossible for the public or the media to uncover evidence about corruption or to protect whistleblowers who outed evidence of misdeeds. It suggested that publication, but also possession of classified information for whatever reason, could be punishable by a jail term of up to 25 years.

Dawes says: "It took place in the international context of growing use and abuse of this kind of legislation, including in those established democracies like the US, and the UK and Canada." Dawes and allies fought off some of the worst aspects of the legislation, but he believes it is now "about as bad as some similar international statutes," but, and here his passion for South Africa comes flooding out, "those should absolutely not be our standard. Our standard in South Africa should be our constitution that requires that any legislation which has the potential to infringe on our basic rights is only acceptable when it is consistent with an open democracy – Section 32 is clear in that regard."

The struggle is not yet over, in his opinion.

"We didn't get it all the way over the line ... so there will be appeals to review the legislation on the basis that it remains inimical to press freedom and freedom of information generally."

The four-year battle over the secrecy bill brought the different elements of South African journalism together, as might have been expected, but the surprise was that it brought them unexpected allies. "The wider victory for freedom of information as a result of this campaign becoming an issue is that it brought public discussion and a broad public engagement, not just in newsrooms and metropolitan salons, but in poor neighbourhoods in remote locations. That is bigger than anything we won on the page," says Dawes.

"I think what it helps us do is to create a climate of support for whistleblowers. Trade unions have got very much involved in the campaign against the legislation because their view is that it is essential to their ability to obtain justice for workers." What has happened, he says, is that this issue has created a set of unusual partners, people who before didn't know each other, and what has happened as a consequence is that "we have taken the fine words of the constitution and made them live on the street and the shop floor."

Being elitist and not covering or caring about issues of the rural poor, or issues beyond the metropolitan elite, is an accusation aimed at journalists around the world. Dawes thinks South Africa's media is doing better than it was at covering stories outside the major cities and from a wider group of people, and part of the reason is social media. He believes the power of Facebook and Twitter to allow people to connect with journalists should not be underestimated. His background in digital media has undoubtedly helped to stimulate M&G's expanded use of web and social media. "We have got to do much more, such as savvy use of new tools to make a difference as well." Social media, and its impact in giving currently excluded communities voices in newspapers and websites should not be underestimated. "Many communities are going to leapfrog print, they are going to leapfrog web and go straight to mobile. Cheap Android phones are coming in and 4G is coming. The potential is absolutely staggering. What we are going to see in five years, we can't even imagine right now."

Not only do journalists need to break away from the same old circles and the media circuit, but they need to do as much as they can to talk to the people who the stories affect, not people speaking for them, he argues. "Part of the circuit can be academics and activists whose voices get in the press instead of the people affected." Asked for an example of the way M&G had done it differently, he mentions a three-page backgrounder that looked at poverty, conflict and discrimination in the platinum belt, voicing people's dissatisfaction with working conditions in the area well ahead of the Marikana belt, the mining protests that ended in the killing of 44 people.

After a long and distinguished history as an investigative journalist it is clear that, despite high office at the paper, Dawes's news nose has not deserted him. He recently came across the sniff of a story while out on his bike. He spotted long queues of people waiting at a water standpoint as he cycled past, started tweeting questions, and uncovered the beginning of a story about water supply problems.

Looking back, as one has a tendency to do ahead of a big move, he rates one of his high points in South African journalism as the story he broke about the ties between a national police commissioner, corrupt business people and the criminal underworld

We do enjoy a robust and free media in South Africa. You can find stories that any government would find challenging

– "It spoke to the criminalisation of the state at a very high level." During his time as editor-in-chief he has shown commitment to supporting that kind of journalism among his team in innovative ways. Not just by encouraging his reporters to go out and spend time on creating good, thorough pieces of work, rather than skimming-off-the-top superficial stories, but also by helping set up a non-profit arm, a centre for investigative journalism. The centre, AmaBhungame, provides investigative journalism training for reporters from around Africa. This approach has borne fruit, says Dawes, by setting the news agenda, not just in South Africa but in surrounding countries, including Zambia and Zimbabwe. With an oppressive news environment for journalists in Zimbabwe, the M&G, under Dawes' leadership, has also expanded its coverage of its neighbour to →

|||||||||||||||||||||||||||||||||||||||||||||||||||||

The Freedom House 2013 report on press freedom cites Zimbabwe's status for press as "not free", with a 77 score, with journalists facing intimidation, attacks and arrests

→ find "stories told that are not being told at home" and started selling papers over the border.

Investigative journalism comes in all shapes, sizes and sections of the paper. Dawes is particularly proud of a fight to keep details of business ownership in the public domain, so that South African companies had to continue to list their shareholders publicly, "something that was set to disappear."

One element of South African media which is in dire need of reform, he argues, is SABC radio, the public broadcaster and main source of news for many thousands of people, particularly in rural communities. "It is in a dire state (newspapers cannot fill the gap) and much more attention should be given to what they are doing." His lament will sound familiar to the critics of public/state news radio in the country Dawes is heading off to, India, where legislation prevents other operators from setting up competitor news radio channels to the government-backed national channel.

Dawes' departure from South Africa has been widely discussed, with many wondering why he is making the leap. He says that media anger about the Protection of State Information bill has not been a factor in him leaving for India: "While I am disappointed and angry that the people who brought us press freedom now seek to restrict it, I am not sad in a way that makes me feel despairing."

"We are going through a very classical process, what happens when a liberation movement has been in power for a while and starts to see its hegemony challenged and then reaches for a convenient lever to limit that challenge."

He points out that this comes from a fraction of the ANC, not all of it, But he also points to Nelson Mandela's legacy as part of that fight for a free press. "Mandela's legacy has been too easily dismissed by too many South Africans, including our political leaders. His legacy is being brought back to us."

And he thinks the move to India and the Hindustan Times, with its 3.7 million readers, will be challenging and exciting: "It is an utterly compelling story, and anyone from a media background would be excited to be part of it. You have remarkable and sometimes difficult economic and social change within a very dynamic political environment," he says, tactfully.

But he is leaving behind a media that he thinks consistently breaks important stories, and is not afraid of invoking government displeasure. "We do enjoy a robust and free media in South Africa. You can open your copy of a paper here and find stories that any government would find challenging."

"We are not prevented in any explicit way from publishing those things, and even the implicit pressures are withstood pretty well."

Now Dawes is leaving South Africa, and heading for India, where media consumption is mind-blowingly massive, but where political influence and corruption are stalking horses. Luckily his enthusiasm for taking on challenges is undimmed. X

©Index
www.indexoncensorship.org

Rachael Jolley is editor of Index on Censorship

A land without justice or truth

42(3): 83/87 | DOI: 10.1177/0306422013501773

In Ingushetia, bungled counter-terrorism operations end in the tragic deaths of innocent civilians. Chechen journalist and editor **Abdulla Duduev** talks to one family about their shocking experience

FOR RUSSIANS, THE North Caucasus is a territory where the rule of law does not apply. This stereotype view is partly true, but not everyone knows why.

People in Chechnya, Ingushetia and Dagestan say they defy laws not because they do not want to abide by them, but because officials who are supposed to uphold the law violate it in outrageous ways. Lawlessness in the Russian military and special services is not new: it dates back to the first Chechen War (1994–96). Authorities responsible for investigating these crimes have repeatedly turned a blind eye to them; in the North Caucasus, it's an everyday reality.

So-called "anti-terrorism special operations" have resulted in the murder and kidnapping of innocent people. Military and law enforcement officers often describe their victims as "gunmen" or accomplices to "terrorists" – they know people who are tortured or killed will not be able to prove them wrong.

Yunus-bek Yevkurov, the president of Ingushetia, uses the same approach. He frequently smears victims of kidnapping – some of whom are still missing and have probably been killed – without any evidence. It's surprising, then, that Yevkurov, a former paratrooper commander and intelligence general, has a reputation as an open politician, a statesman who can meet human rights defenders and have a friendly chat with them over a cup of tea. Some people praise him for suggesting he is not completely in charge. He regularly points out that law enforcement officials and the army are accountable to Moscow, but not to him.

To this day, Adam's relatives do not know anything about his fate

Yet Yevkurov himself admits this is not entirely true. "When I say law enforcements are not accountable to me, it does not mean they act on the territory of our republic without endorsement from the authorities. We control all the special operations," he told Gazeta.ru on 24 April 2013.

When asked about an incident in a village earlier that month, he said: "I knew about the special operation in Dolakovo; I knew who the special enforcement officers would be searching for there. More than that, the beginning and the end of the operation were →

ABOVE: Military checkpoint on the border between Ingushetia and Chechnya, 2000

→ reported to me directly, because I am in charge here," he added.

So what happened in Dolakovo?

"Damn, this is the wrong house!"

At the break of dawn on 8 April 2013, a military operation took place in Kombileevsaya Street in the village of Dolakovo, complete with armed vehicles. It was as if a siege was under way and the army had been instructed to intervene. A local inhabitant, Khavazh Ozdoev, 31, always left his house at number 35 very early; he worked in a boiler room at a local school and had to ensure classrooms were warm before children arrived.

That morning he left his house as usual, but as he turned to close the gate behind him, a burst of submachine gunfire took him down. Khavazh was killed on the spot.

Adam Ozdoev, Khavazh's younger brother, ran out of the house when he heard the noise. He says that when he saw a group of armed military personnel and his brother lying dead, he ran off. As he did, he saw his cousin Artur Pliev arriving. Artur lived nearby and had been preparing for his morning prayer when he heard the gun go off. He rushed to his relatives' house.

Adam shouted to Artur to run away, but they were brought down by a new round of gunshots. Artur Pliev was shot dead; Adam Ozdoev was wounded.

Zareta Ozdoeva, Khavazh and Adam's sister saw what happened and rushed to the gates of their house, despite the fact that the soldiers shouted at her and warned her not to approach.

"Who are you and what are you doing?" she cried.

"Is this Mestoev?" asked one of the soldiers.

"No, this is my brother Khavazh Ozdoev," Zareta replied.

The soldier told her that Khavazh had opened fire first. She asked him to look at her brother's body.

"He did not have a weapon, and he was lying with his face down and his arms stretched up. He had clearly been shot in the back, there were bullet holes in his back and his leg, and there was another one on his head. All in all, I heard more than 20 shots in our yard," said Zareta Ozdoeva when I spoke to her.

According to Zareta, she wanted to turn her brother's body over to show the soldiers that he had been unarmed, but they wouldn't let her approach him. Shortly after, they took the body away. Later, a video appeared on the internet, showing Khavazh Ozdoev's body in a different pose – and there was a gun with a silencer behind him.

After the murders, the military used explosives to destroy the house. Zareta persuaded them to search it first, however, to see that there was nothing dangerous there, that there had been no reason to attack her brother. She says the soldiers were afraid to enter the house, and agreed only when Zareta said she would lead them in as a human shield.

"One of them was in touch with somebody with a portable radio and reported that everything was fine. I showed them all the rooms in the house, and when we approached the garage, one of them pulled a terrible face and shouted at his radio 'Damn,

this is the wrong house! We needed the second house from the left corner of the quarter, and this one is the second from the right!'"

They forced Zareta and her mother to leave the house, and then proceeded to rob it. Minutes before they were afraid to enter – but once they saw there was no danger, they began looting, despite it being "the wrong house".

Adam Ozdoev, the wounded brother, was taken to the central clinical hospital of Nazran, the largest city in Ingushetia. Witnesses later told his family he was accompanied by two law enforcement officers; they allowed doctors to dress his wounds and took him to an undisclosed place directly afterwards. To this day, Adam's relatives do not know anything about his fate.

Human lives become statistics used to demonstrate how effective the government has been in "the war on terror"

The Ozdoevs' mother, Ayshat, is disabled; she cannot walk without assistance. She came to Ingushetia as a refugee 20 years ago, following conflict between the Ossetians and the Ingush in North Ossetia. She brought up her daughter and two sons alone – and lost her sons and her nephew in just one morning. All three worked at a local school. Adam Ozdoev taught information science. Artur Pliev was a chief accountant.

"My children grew up in front of my eyes. All our neighbours knew them and knew they were doing nothing criminal or illegal; all the village saw them every day going to work, and coming back from their school," said Ayshat as she tried to hold back tears that rolled from her eyes, filled with pain.

She does not know where to seek justice. She is desperate, and she does not trust or believe the federal or regional authorities. →

ABOVE: Zareta and Ayshat Ozdoev

→ Despite her loss and deep sorrow, when I spoke to her she still had some faith in Yunus-bek Yevkurov, even though he failed to apologise for the murders of these innocent people. It is not normal practice for the military to give reasons or excuse mistakes that occur during special operations, even if these mistakes cost lives.

On 18 April, Yevkurov agreed to meet Ayshat Ozdoeva. He asked her to bring her son Adam, who authorities claim she is hiding. Yevkurov promised to rehabilitate him if he surrendered. An officer of the Federal Security Service (FSB) Pavel Chernov, who was in charge of the "special operation" in Dolakovo, was also present at the meeting. As he started to tell the military's account of events – that they had to kill Khavazh

Ozdoev because he had opened fire first – Ayshat broke down.

"Why are you telling these lies? Aren't you ashamed?" she cried.

This was the end of the meeting. The elderly woman was escorted out of the president's office.

Zareta Ozdoeva says her mother returned from the meeting exhausted and run down; she had been in poor health before, and her condition worsened.

This story's ending is quite common. The words of enforcement officers are accepted as the truth, even after they loot a house and kill an unarmed man, even when that unarmed man is later pictured with a gun next to his body that had not been there before. A couple of weeks later, a new photograph was posted on the internet: this time the photograph shows Khavazh Ozdoev's body next to a machine gun.

But Yevkurov is too busy to question these suspicious miracles. In his interview to Gazeta.ru he described the Ozdoevs as "people with weapons" and "accomplices of clandestine gangs". He told journalists that Adam Ozdoev ran away from the hospital and is being hidden by his relatives. In the same interview, he complained: "nobody believes us when we say these people were planning an act of terror."

A vicious circle

For people in the region, it is a vicious circle. They suffer enormously because of the blatant lawlessness of law enforcement and military authorities.

When a person is kidnapped or killed, the victim's relatives appeal to the police. Often their complaints are not even registered properly. They go to human rights defenders and independent journalists, who help them complete the formalities of their legal appeals, make the cases public and spread the word. But relatives do not have much of an incentive to tell their stories: in the majority of cases it does not lead to the triumph of justice.

It is for the relatives of victims to search for those who were kidnapped. Officers who are involved in murders, tortures and kidnappings are not brought to account. Instead, they are promoted. Human lives become nothing but statistics the military and the regional authorities use to demonstrate how effective they've been in "the war on terror". As a result, state funding for anti-terrorism troops and special services is increased.

Victims remain alone with their grief and pain. Some wait quietly in hope that justice will be restored one day; others go down the road of long and exhausting trials and using all the legal mechanisms to hand, sometimes taking their cases to the European Court of Human Rights. But there are those who decide to seek a form of justice with weapons in their hands. The military authorities seem to welcome this response the most, not least because it boosts their careers and builds their wealth.

This vicious circle is so hard to break. ☒

©Abdulla Duduev
www.indexoncensorship.org

Abdulla Duduev is the editor-in-chief of DOSH, a magazine published in Russian and English and distributed throughout the North Caucasus

Thought police

42(3): 88/92 | DOI: 10.1177/0306422013500739

When independent pollsters reported that the Russian government was not as popular as it might like the public to think, they were labelled as foreign agents. It's no crime to tell people the truth, says **Peter Kellner**.

LET US START with basic principles. A crucial feature of any true democracy is the ability of citizens to make their voices heard – by the country's leaders and by each other: not just in elections but all the time. Well-conducted opinion polls are one way to measure public opinion. They are certainly not the only way but for some tasks they are indispensable. They are the most scientific way to gauge the level of support for politicians, parties and policies – and whether that support is rising or falling. It follows that any attempt to curb the right to conduct and report opinion polls is not just a matter of business regulation but an assault on a vital democratic freedom.

This is why an apparently narrow controversy in Russia is so important. One of

It found that 51% of Russians agreed with the nickname of the governing party, United Russia, as "the party of swindlers and thieves"

Russia, freedom and the media

....

Andrei Aliaksandrau reports on crackdowns and censorship in Russia over the last 18 months.

"It's 2016 and when a Russian MP learnt there was nothing more to ban, he just went out and kicked a dog." This joke reflects the general impression of the latest legal initiatives taken by the Russian authorities.

The scale and pace at which the Duma, the lower chamber of the national parliament, adopts repressive laws has earned it a nickname of "a crazy printer". The "crazy printing" started after Vladimir Putin's return as president in May 2012. The comeback wasn't particularly glorious, as it was marked with mass protests that showed Putin had lost his wide popularity and thus had to seek support from more conservative parts of society. The way to win their hearts and remain in power is quite typical of any authoritarian regime: you need to find enemies, both external and internal, and switch public attention from real problems to fighting those foes.

"A series of laws passed in Russia over the last year have changed the very fundamental principles of the state and its relationship with society. In fact they have deprived citizens of their constitutional

the country's leading independent research agencies, Levada Centre, faces closure. On 15 May 2013, state prosecutors warned Levada that it "violates federal legislation" by accepting research commissions from abroad. Such work (say the prosecutors) makes the centre a "foreign agent". Under a law passed in November 2012, this needs to be registered. The centre has not joined any such register and is liable to fines of up to half a million roubles. One does not need to suffer from acute paranoia to detect a familiar pattern – a nervous government exploiting its control of the legal system to use administrative measures in order to silence an independent voice.

How have things come to this? A brief chronology leads us towards the answer.

- In the 1960s, Professor Yuri Levada taught sociology at Moscow State University. As part of the slight loosening of Soviet oppression, as Nikita Khruschev sought to distance himself from the horrors of Stalinism, Levada was allowed to establish an institute to conduct limited surveys.
- In 1972 his institute was closed down. He was one of many victims of the Brezhnev

era. Some of Levada's findings had caused offence in high places, such as his discovery that few people read Pravda's long and tedious editorials praising the Soviet system.

- In 1987, during Mikhail Gorbachev's "glasnost" phase, Levada was able to try again; he established VTSIOM, the "all-Union Centre for the Study of Public Opinion". It was technically government-owned but established a reputation for independence and accuracy during the turbulent years that saw the downfall of the Soviet system and the rise of Boris Yeltsin.
- In 2003, the government exploited its powers as owners to clear out VTSIOM's board of directors. Levada and some of his colleagues resigned and established their own, fully independent, Levada Centre.
- For the past decade, the centre has conducted surveys for a variety of Russian and overseas clients. Levada himself died in 2006, but his centre lives on. It produces a detailed annual, state-of-the-nation survey that is vital reading for anyone who wants to track the mood of the Russian people. Among its clients →

rights to freedom of expression, assembly and association," says Yury Dzibladze, President of the Centre for the Development of Democracy and Human Rights.

One of the most notorious laws passed has been the so-called "foreign agent law". It requires NGOs that receive foreign funding to register as "foreign agents" if they are involved in "political activities". Failure to comply leaves NGOs and their leaders open to fines and possible prison terms. The problem is that the authorities define as "politics" anything that can potentially influence public opinion. A wide range of NGOs, from human rights groups to a national park dealing with the protection of cranes, received warnings from local prosecutors' offices.

A common issue with the latest legislation in Russia is that laws contain ambiguous provisions allowing their selective implementation, and some of them do not comply with international standards.

Defamation was re-criminalised in July 2012 after being excluded from the Criminal Code just seven months before under President Medvedev. "Propaganda of non-traditional sexual relationships" is banned. The new repressive legislation also includes further restrictions on the right to peaceful protest, a ban on "harming of religious feelings →

ABOVE: Challenges to government positions have provoked severe repercussions in Putin's Russia

→ are serious western institutions such as the Ford Foundation and George Soros's Open Society Institute. These are openly acknowledged.

As an independent institution, the centre has upset government leaders by showing what the public really thinks of them. In April, it found that 51 per cent of Russians agreed with the nickname of the governing party, United Russia, as "the party of swindlers and thieves". It regularly shows that President Putin is less popular than the government claims.

On the other hand, being independent, the centre also produces findings that sometimes support the government position and show that most Russians reject liberal values. For example, the centre's April survey found that 73 per cent want a ban on public displays or

→ of believers", introduction of a black list of websites with 'harmful content' and the "anti-Magnitsky law", which forbids NGOs to receive funds from US citizens and also blocks the adoption of Russian children by Americans. The law was introduced after the US passed the Magnitsky Act, which blacklisted Russian officials linked to human rights abuses.

"Law making from the Duma over the last year makes me question the common sense of Russian MPs. It looks like they believe they can regulate everything by law, from street rallies to sexual relationships of citizens," says Dmitry Makarov, a co-chair of the International Youth Human Rights Movement.

Freedom of the media is deteriorating.

Freedom House rated Russia 176th out of 196 countries in their Freedom of the Press 2013 index, and there are no signs of improvement. Russia continues to be one of the deadliest places for journalists. According to the Committee to Protect Journalists, 54 reporters have been killed in Russia since 1992, with 16 cases still unsolved.

Impunity remains a significant problem. The killers of Natalia Estemirova, Abdulmalik Akhmedilov, Khadzhimurad Kamalov and other prominent investigative reporters have never been prosecuted; nor have the organisers of Anna Politkovskaya's murder.

Akhmednabi Akhmednabiev, a well-known Russian journalist

justification of homosexuality – which meant that there was majority support for a law, passed in June, to fine people who "propagate" homosexuality. And by two-to-one Russians thought the two-year prison sentences imposed on the feminist punk rock group, Pussy Riot, were "reasonable" rather than "excessive". Only 9 per cent thought the Pussy Riot members should not have been prosecuted at all.

In short, the Levada Centre cannot be accused of being a western Trojan Horse seeking to distort public opinion in pursuit of a hostile, liberal agenda. Its "crime" seems to be no more and no less than its determination to tell the truth about public opinion.

Now, in theory, the centre might appear able to withstand the prosecutors' assault. Just 3 per cent of the centre's income comes from foreign sources. That, though, understates the threat. In an email to me, Lev Gudkov, the centre's director, said that "it frightens our Russian and foreign business partners reluctant to make enemies with the Kremlin; it stigmatises us as 'foreign agents' with a considerable sector of Russian public opinion."

He added: "We are now in the process of juridical consultations, trying to avoid a possible closure". One option is to file a lawsuit asserting that the "foreign agents" law violates Russia's own constitution. However, Professor Gudkov fears that this challenge would take too long and that, meanwhile, their research activities would collapse. A quicker solution would be to accept the prosecutors' demand that the centre accepts that it "influences public opinion and therefore does not constitute research but political activity". Gudkov says that demand is unacceptable: "it is humiliating as it forces us to slander ourselves."

It frightens our Russian and foreign business partners reluctant to make enemies with the Kremlin; it stigmatises us as "foreign agents"

The good news is that, following professional support at home and news stories in the West about the centre's plight, notably in the New York Times, Russia's government has acted cautiously. Gudkov told me: "We have not faced any harassment from the government or similar agencies. On the contrary, there is an →

who reported on human rights violations in the Caucasus, recently joined this list; he was shot dead near his house in a suburb of Makhachkala on 9 July 2013.

The legal framework of media activities is also getting harsher. As well as adding libel back into the Criminal Code, other legislative challenges have included a law on high treason that endangers Russian journalists who work for the international media (it prohibits providing certain information to foreign countries) and a law that forbids the media from using obscene words.

Extensive online censorship, including blocking and filtering of online content, happens, as does surveillance of Russians' online activities. SORM, a nationwide surveillance system, operated with Deep Packet Inspection (DPI) technology, allows the state security force not only to control but even to intrude into the internet traffic of any internet user in Russia, without any special permit or court decision.

A crackdown on rights and freedoms of Russian citizens is just one part of the story. Repressive law-making is a trend in other countries of the region as well, especially as Russia aims to set the tone on the international stage. The regimes of Belarus, Azerbaijan, China, Iran and other members of the "Authoritarian →

→ unprecedented professional solidarity campaign, including all the major academic organisations in Russia and some abroad."

There is, then, a window of opportunity. Russia insists that it is a democracy – new and imperfect, to be sure, but edging away from the old, authoritarian methods of the Soviet era. It may yet conclude that the gains to be made from closing down the Levada Centre are not worth the opprobrium of being seen to silence its work.

For this reason, I have abandoned my normal reluctance to sign petitions and round-robin letters. I have registered my support for a Europe-wide campaign to back Levada, and urge others to do the same: www.zeitschrift-osteuropa.de/support-levada/de 🗵

©Peter Kellner
www.indexoncensorship.org

Peter Kellner is president of YouGov

→ Club" learn from each other and act together to try to block international human rights mechanisms. They even try to re-define the very concept of human rights, claiming it is nothing but a matter of internal affairs for each and every separate state. 🗵

©Andrei Aliaksandrau
www.indexoncensorship.org

Andrei Aliaksandrau is Belarus and OSCE programme officer at Index on Censorship

HAVE CHANGES IN RUSSIA AFFECTED FREE EXPRESSION?

OPINION

42(3): 93/94 | DOI: 10.1177/0306422013505586

Leading human rights advocates give their opinions

....

Dmitry Makarov
CO-CHAIR OF THE INTERNATIONAL YOUTH HUMAN RIGHTS MOVEMENT

THE SO-CALLED "FOREIGN agents law" was introduced so the authorities of Russia can restrict under the pretext of "national interests" any civic activity aimed at influencing public opinion, including defending human rights, protection of the environment or fighting corruption. Human rights are considered to be an issue of "national sovereignty", and no external player is allowed to "intrude". In fact it means Russia challenges the very fundamental principles of the post-war system of human rights that is based on the belief that human rights are universal. Attempts to redefine human rights by the Russian authorities are dangerous as at the moment they do not face strong opposition from the international community and can potentially affect the whole system of international relations.

....

Natalia Taubina
DIRECTOR OF PUBLIC VERDICT FOUNDATION

THE WAY THE prosecutor's office defines our activities contradicts the standards of human rights we are defending. Our traditional work is declared to be politics. According to the authorities, we can continue supporting victims of torture, but we cannot publicly speak about it. Or we can criticise reforms of the police, but do it invisibly to citizens. If we follow the logic of the prosecutor's office, we should refuse our profession and stop being human rights defenders. This is in fact a ban for publicity and prohibition of attempts to influence the state, which is an integral part of human rights work in any open and democratic society. We do have a choice; we can continue being human rights defenders, but only in the status of "foreign agents." Our moral obligations to people we help do not allow us to agree to this status, because we act in their interests, and by no means in the interests of some non-existent "foreign principals".

....

Lyudmila Alexeeva
CHAIR OF THE MOSCOW HELSINKI GROUP, THE OLDEST HUMAN RIGHTS ORGANISATION IN RUSSIA, IN THE GUARDIAN

IT IS PRECISELY to destroy civil society – and primarily the human rights groups that form its backbone – that a series of repressive →

→ laws were adopted in 2012 by Russia's Duma, elected fraudulently and obedient to Putin. One of these laws requires that NGOs which receive funding from abroad and "engage in politics" voluntarily register as "foreign agents." This demand is the equivalent of Nazi Germany's demand that Jews don a yellow star. This law is directed against human rights organisations that have to receive financing from foreign donors in order to maintain their independence – since neither the Russian government nor big business will support organisations whose goal is to protect citizens from violations of their rights by the state.

....

Elena Panfilova
HEAD OF CENTRE TRANSPARENCY INTERNATIONAL, RUSSIA, POSTED ON FACEBOOK

BY ABOUT THE end of the autumn there won't remain a single independent NGO left in our country. In the end there is a choice for everyone to make: either to close down one's own organisation or to be prosecuted and face up to two years in prison. There are no other variants. Not for anyone. I think that not everyone understands this, but this is the bottom line. ⌧

www.indexoncensorship.org

Reign of terror

42(3): 95/98 | DOI: 10.1177/0306422013502443

In Honduras, journalists are threatened, attacked and even killed for their reporting. In the run-up to the November general election, **Dina Meza** calls for the international community to act

WITH ONE OF the highest murder rates in the world, Honduras is also one of the most dangerous countries to be a journalist. In the last decade, at least 32 media workers have lost their lives and many more have faced violent attacks and intimidation, regardless of whether they work for mainstream newspapers and broadcasting companies owned by the country's elite or for alternative media and community radio stations. In the run-up to the 24 November 2013 national elections, this repression has escalated. By repeatedly failing to punish those who use violence against journalists and activists, the Honduran government has effectively given criminals a licence to kill.

It's vital that, as Honduras prepares to go to the polls, international human rights and election observers highlight and document these crimes, offering support to those who are risking their lives to document appalling human rights abuses in the country.

One of the most shocking cases is that of television journalist Anibal Barrow, who was abducted on 24 June 2013. His dismembered body was discovered days later, sending the country's journalists into a state of panic. On the day of his abduction, Barrow had invited members of the Partido de Libertad y Refundacion (the Party of Freedom and Renewal, or LIBRE) to speak on his popular news programme. Set up in response to the 2009 coup that deposed President Manuel Zelaya, the left-wing coalition is predictably unpopular with Porfirio Lobo Sosa's government. The murder was thought to be linked to drug cartels in the region.

Barrow's murder has served as a warning, not only for journalists but also for people working to bring about change via the ballot box – including those calling for the introduction of a constituent national assembly to tackle systematic looting and corruption and to help reinstate some semblance of rule of law.

Bullets have become the sole response to any attempt to exercise the right to freedom of expression

Those reporting on human rights violations, drug trafficking, organised crime, US intervention in Honduran politics and corruption are clearly vulnerable. Land issues are also highly contentious topics. Whether it's the destruction of the environment for profit, particularly by mining and hydro-electric companies, land ownership or land-grabbing, these live issues galvanise communities and journalists alike, who use both traditional media and social networks to spread information. Other human →

ABOVE: The son of slain journalist Anibal Barrow pays tribute to his father at his funeral in San Pedro Sula, Honduras, 10 July 2013

→ rights advocates, including those working to protect and promote the rights of women, indigenous and black people and lesbian, gay, bi-sexual and transgender communities, have also been repressed and silenced.

A new reign of terror is undeniably under way. Paramilitaries and hired killers have emerged on the scene, making it easy for the state to avoid responsibility for the increased violence. Convictions are rare. According to the National Committee on Human Rights, 97 per cent of crimes committed against journalists, human rights workers and activists since the military coup have gone unpunished. In a democracy, criminal inves-

tigations would be the appropriate means to bring these culprits to justice, but in what is an essentially failed state with a collapsed infrastructure, anyone who is determined to speak out risks their life.

Since 2009, the country's human rights record has deteriorated. There are claims that organised crime, drug trafficking and corruption within the police force are on the increase. Serious social and economic problems persist; poverty has increased, with around 300,000 people falling below the poverty line since the coup. While President Porfirio Lobo Sosa has been in power, at least 29 journalists have

Honduras's murdered journalists, 2003–2013

Anibal Barrow, Globo TV, Cortes – 24 June 2013

Celin Orlando Acosta Zelaya, freelance, Olancho – 31 January 2013

Angel Edgardo Lopez Fiallos, journalism student, Francisco Morazan – 8 November 2012

Julio Cesar Cassaleno, Direction Nacional de Transito (Transport) – 28 August 2012

Jose Noel Canales Lagos, Hondudiario and SEPROC, Tegucigalpa – 10 August 2012

Adonis Felipe Bueso Gutierrez, Radio Naranja, Cortes – 8 July 2012

Erick Martinez, Asociacion Kukulcan, Francisco Morazan – 7 May 2012

Noel Alexander Valladares, Maya TV, Francisco Morazan – 23 April 2012

Fausto Elio Valle, Radio Alegre, Colon – 11 March 2012

Fabiola Almendares Borjas, journalism student, Cortes – 1 March 2012

Luz Marina Paz, Honduran News Channel, Francisco Morazan – 6 December 2011

Medardo Flores, Radio Uno, Cortes – 9 September 2011

Nery Jeremias Orellana, Radio Joconguera, Lempira – 14 July 2011

Adan Benitez, 45TV and Teleceiba Canal 7, Atlantida – 5 July 2011

Luis Mendoza, Macrosistema Company and Canal 24, Danli – 19 May 2011

Hector Francisco Medina Polanco, Omega Visión, Yoro – 10 May 2011

Henry Orlando Suazo, HRN, Atlantida – 28 December 2010

Israel Diaz Zelaya, Radio Internacional, Cortes – 24 August 2010

Luis Arturo Mondragon, Canal 19, El Paraiso –14 June 2010

Luis Chevez Hernandez, Radio W105, San Pedro Sula – 09 April 2010

Victor Manuel Juarez Vasquez, Canal 4 de Juticalpa, Olancho – 26 March 2010

Bayardo Mairena, Canal 4 de Juticalpa, Olancho – 26 March 2010

Nahum Palacios, Canal 5 de Aguan, Colon – 14 March 2010

David Meza, El Patio and Radio America, Atlantida – 11 March 2010

Joseph Hernandez, Canal 51, Francisco Morazan – 1 March 2010

Nicolas Asfura, Construction Company, Francisco Morazan – 17 February 2010

Gabriel Fino Noriega, Radio America, Atlantida – 3 July 2009

Osman Rodrigo Lopez, Canal 45, Francisco Morazan – 19 April 2009

Rafael Munguia, Radio Cadena Voces, Cortes – 1 April 2009

Bernardo Rivera Paz, Freelancer, Copan – 14 March 2009

Fernando Gonzalez, Radio Mega FM 92.7, Santa Barbara – 1 January 2008

Carlos Salgado, Radio Cadena Voces, Morazan – 18 October 2007

German Rivas, Corporacion Maya Vision Canal 7, Copan – 26 November 2003

To date, no one has been prosecuted for the above crimes

Source: Honduras Human Rights Commissioner

lost their lives. In contrast, three journalists were killed during the period of democracy (2003–8). Before the coup, journalists often received threatening "farewell" telephone calls at their workplaces. This practice is now relegated to the past – bullets have become the sole response to any attempt to exercise the right to freedom of expression.

As far as international observers are concerned, the gravity of the situation is unprecedented, leading human rights delegations to visit Honduras to assess the situation. Among them was United Nations Special Rapporteur on the promotion and protection of the right to freedom of opinion and expression Frank La Rue, who visited the country in August 2012. Speaking about his visit, La Rue said that when journalists face violence, harassment, threats and violent attacks in any country, the government should immediately launch a full investigation into these crimes and punish those responsible. In Honduras, La Rue said, the "absence of justice constitutes an impunity in and of itself, and impunity is one of the principal causes of the continuing and renewed violence". →

He called on the government to establish a council – made up of members of the press and civil society, as well as representatives from the defence and the interior ministries – to protect human rights and freedom of expression. The body should have direct access to the most senior governmental authorities, including the president and the security services, and should be in a position to manage its own budget so that it has the power to put effective methods of protection in place.

Yet Porfirio Lobo Sosa's government has still not moved from words to deeds. It has not undertaken the necessary actions to promote freedom of expression across the country, not only for journalists but for the entire population. And because of this, attacks on the press have escalated from simple threats to the most horrific crimes.

Most people are not prepared to risk their lives. So when sharing information, they are likely to do so anonymously. This places enormous pressure on journalists, who are left to claim responsibility for reporting on human rights violations. In such a climate of fear, many have already discontinued their television and radio programmes; others have gone into exile; the rest practise self-censorship.

Freedom of expression is a cornerstone of democracy. It is time for the international community to take an instrumental role in resolving the situation in Honduras, acknowledging that its problems no longer simply constitute an internal issue but have implications and reverberations globally.

In the meantime, how many more will be gunned down and serve as symbols of ignominy and impunity? It is still not too late for us to act. ☒

©Dina Meza
www.indexoncensorship.org

Dina Meza is a journalist and activist in Honduras

Translated by Amanda Hopkinson

War on the media

42(3): 99/104 | DOI: 10.1177/0306422013500206

Journalists throughout the country are forced to choose between silence or death threats, assassination attempts and exile. Ahead of next year's election, can freedom of the Colombian press survive, asks **Jeremy Dear**

"I WAS URINATING when it happened," said Ricardo Calderón, one of Colombia's leading investigative journalists, reliving his narrow escape from a mafia-style assassination attempt on 1 May 2013.

On his way home from conducting an interview, Calderón, an editor at Colombia's weekly news magazine Semana, got out of his car and was standing behind it at the side of the road when he heard the screech of tyres. A man shouted his name and fired a gun at him five times. He escaped by diving into a ditch.

It's clear that the bullets were meant to kill Calderón, who had in recent years played a key role in exposing major human rights scandals – his most recent investigation had been into military officers convicted of committing atrocities; despite being held at a detention centre, they had been allowed to leave as they pleased and carry on with outside business activities. But the bullets also sent a message to Colombia's increasingly beleaguered journalists: keep your noses out.

In May and June 2013, Cuba played host to a series of peace talks between the head negotiator of Colombia's largest guerrilla organisation, the Revolutionary Armed Forces of Colombia (FARC), and the government. But even as the talks were taking place, the number of attacks against journalists rose.

Across Colombia, criminal gangs, paramilitary organisations, narco-traffickers and local and national politicians don't hesitate to threaten reporters whom they believe are jeopardising their interests.

More than 90 journalists currently receive some form of security from the Colombian Ministry of the Interior's National Protection Unit. Thirty-four of them carry out their interviews and investigations under the protection of armed bodyguards. And while many welcome the increased protection given

Without measures to tackle impunity, self-censorship will become more widespread

to individual journalists, few believe these measures alone are adequate to tackle the widespread threat to freedom of expression.

In the days following Calderón's attack, police uncovered an assassination plot against three prominent Colombian journalists. A hitman had been hired to kill investigative journalist Gonzalo Guillén, columnist León Valencia and researcher Ariel Ávila. The three believed the threats were directly related to an investigation and documentary they had been working on that revealed links between corrupt politicians and criminal gangs, including details of →

→ 126 local and national politicians whose election campaigns had been financed by such gangs.

Already a number of Guillén's sources – including the wife of the former mayor of Barrancas, who himself was assassinated – had been murdered after speaking with him. Another source had been killed by a death squad in La Guajira province after revealing details of local criminal activity; the brother of one of his bodyguards was shot dead. Ávila, Guillén and Valencia have now gone into exile.

But perhaps the clearest message came six days later, on 7 May. Eight journalists in Cesar were threatened with murder. They had been investigating land seizures carried out by paramilitary groups at the same time as a group of displaced peasants asking for restitution had been killed.

The threat was published in a leaflet, signed by the paramilitary Anti-Land Restitution Army and distributed to newsrooms. It featured an image of an automatic weapon and mentioned the journalists by name, referring to them as "military targets". They were ordered to stop their investigations immediately and given 24 hours to leave the area or be killed. "If you continue to stick your noses in cases of land restitution and victims, you will be next," the leaflet warned. The eight journalists are currently receiving government protection.

New war on the media

In this new war on Colombia's media, these incidents are the tip of the iceberg. There were 158 direct attacks on journalists in 2012 alone. Fernando Londoño, a radio talk show host and former politician, was injured and his driver and bodyguard killed in a targeted bombing. Freelance journalist Guillermo Quiroz Delgado died after being arrested while covering a street protest in Sucre department; there were allegations of police brutality. Collective threats were made against ten reporters in Santa Marta;

six others were forcibly displaced in Antioquia. Community radio stations have been bombed. The list goes on.

In recent months, the attacks have increased. Journalists covering the April 2013 coffee workers' strike faced systematic violence at the hands of the mobile anti-riot force (ESMAD); a radio station was forced off air after its equipment was destroyed. Several journalists were hospitalised, and a national TV crew had its cameras smashed by police officers. In Neiva, security forces stormed the offices of the Colombia Informa news service on the pretext of searching for explosives allegedly used by strikers. The news service had regularly reported on police abuse of demonstrators. In August 2013, journalists were targeted while covering clashes between protesters and police during a country-wide national strike.

Among dozens of other registered threats and attacks, Paola Osorio, a radio journalist and presenter, was wounded when attackers threw a grenade at her station. Two of her colleagues were kidnapped. Crime reporters in the Monteria region were given 48 hours to leave the city or face death.

Self-censorship

In late April 2013, a security conference bringing together hundreds of journalists from Mexico, Honduras and Colombia reached a consensus: for journalists, staying alive and unharmed must be their top priority. But in order to achieve this, too many journalists and media outlets have no choice but to resort to self-censorship.

"Threats and attacks are on the increase against journalists, human rights campaigners, union representatives and community activists. Protection measures will have no effect without a mechanism to fight impunity that is capable of dealing with these circumstances effectively," Reporters Sans Frontières said after the attack on Ricardo Calderón.

Julio Cesar Mesa
Vargas, 24 Años

Jaime Castillo
Peña, 42 Años

Jaime Estiven Valencia
Sanabria, 16 Años

Julián Oviedo
Monroy, 19 Años

Daniel Alexander
Martínez, 22 Años

Joaquín Castro
Vásquez, 27 Años

Jaime Estiven Valen

ABOVE: Demonstration in support of displaced citizens and calling for land restitution, Bogotá, 6 March 2012

Journalist Robert Nieto agrees. He was threatened by a local official in Caucasia, Antioquia, while investigating the town government's spending of US$1 million on a now abandoned, half-built library. The threats were reinforced by former paramilitaries, now operating as criminal gangs, who, he says, work hand in hand with the politicians.

"We can register events, but investigative journalism is off limits," Nieto, editor of Región al Día, told the Committee to Protect Journalists (CPJ). "We need to have good journalism, but it's dangerous to write about alliances between local authorities and the criminal gangs."

Antioquia is one of the most dangerous regions of Colombia for journalists. Since 2009, FLIP has registered 31 threats against reporters, forcing some journalists into exile.

The result has been a virtual blackout of in-depth news coverage. Following extortion threats and a grenade attack on its studio, local radio station Caucasia Stereo FM now no longer reports on allegations of links between police, public officials and gangs.

→

Attacks on journalists

10 July 2013: Two correspondents from Teleantioquia Noticias in Bajo Cauca receive death threats

16 May 2013: Radio talk show host and former politician Fernando Londoño is targeted in a bomb attack. His driver and bodyguard are killed

15 May 2013: Police uncover an assassination plot against three journalists, Gozalo Guillen, León Valencia and Ariel Ávila

9 May 2013: RCN Television's press vehicles and equipment attacked in Bogota following coverage of police operation to seize contraband goods

7 May 2013: Eight journalists in Cesar receive death threats following the publication of reports on land seizures

1 May 2013: Investigative journalist Ricardo Calderón escapes assassination attempt after reporting on corruption and illegal activity among Colombia's political elite

May 2013: Journalist Rober Nieto is threatened by a local official in Antioquia, reported to be one of the most dangerous places in the country for journalists. He had been investigating local government spending at the time of the threat

3-4 March 2013: Armed and masked men in Tolima threaten Rodrigo Callejas, a reporter with Región Al Día, and TV journalists from Telecafe following coverage of coffee growers strike

28 February 2013: Writer Germán Uribe is attacked and sustains serious injuries at his home in Subachoque

27 February 2013: Police officers in Huila detonate tear gas grenades inside the offices of Radio Garzon. Journalists Humbertos Sosa, Angel Vargas, Luz Angela Rodriguez are among those injured

28 January 2013: Crime reporters Amilkar Alvear and Jairo Cassiani receive death threats after reporting on the activities of a criminal gang in the Monteria region; they are given 48 hours to leave the city

November 2012: Freelance journalist Guillermo Quiroz Delgado is arrested while covering a street protest. He dies in custody

3 August 2012: A grenade is thrown at a community radio station, wounding journalist Paola Osorio. The previous month, two of Osorio's colleagues had been kidnapped

As of July 2013, 90 journalists are receiving state protection. It is recommended that they use bodyguards in order to carry out their work.

In 2012, there were 158 direct attacks on journalists.

Of the 140 journalists killed in Colombia between 1977 and 2011, only 12 per cent of cases have resulted in sentences.

A recent survey of 700 journalists found 79 per cent of them admitting that they engaged in self-censorship

Sources: Antonio Nariño Project, BBC, CPJ, FECOLPER, FLIP, IFJ, Knight Center for Journalism, OIDHACO, RSF, Reuters, Source Association de Periodistas de Antioquia

→ After its director received seven death threats on his mobile phone, another radio station in nearby Tarazá axed the town's only local news programme and now only plays music. Two government bodyguards accompany Leiderman Ortiz, editor of the local monthly newspaper La Verdad del Pueblo, 24 hours a day after a grenade was thrown at his house and he received two telephone death threats.

Caucasia Mayor José Nadín Arabia unwittingly summed up the situation: "The criminal gangs pressure everyone who writes negative things about them. But reporters no longer publish much about the gangs."

The government lauds the fact that fewer journalists have been killed in the past two years; some international organisations draw encouragement from this relative success. It's true that there is a better funded protection scheme than ever before, but Colombian journalism associations, including FLIP and the country's journalist union FECOLPER, together with international press freedom groups like CPJ and the International Federation of Journalists, say this is simply not enough to guarantee freedom of expression. CPJ's 2012 annual report states that "widespread self-censorship had made the press less of a target".

Members of the media say the statistics only tell part of the story. "The Colombian government says with pride that the number of journalists murdered has dropped, which is true, but not because Colombia is more democratic or because we are more accepting of dissident thought, or of criticism," says Hollman Morris, former presenter of the human rights documentary series Contravia and now director of a Bogotá-based TV station. He too has had to seek temporary exile and protection in the face of death threats. Fewer journalists are being murdered, he says, "because journalists are practising self-censorship". Journalist Claudia Julieta Duque, who went through a seven-year campaign of intimidation and harassment, told me that it is no longer necessary to kill journalists – a climate of fear that breeds self-censorship is well established. In addition, there is widespread belief among journalists that more politicians, corrupt businesses and gangs are resorting to the courts and using libel laws to silence journalists.

There has been little in the way of positive indications of change – despite the arrest warrants issued against seven former senior state security agents for their part in the campaign of "psychological torture" against Claudia Julieta Duque – but the impunity levels for 2012 (the most recent figures available) remain unchanged. With regard to the Anti-Land Restitution Army, the government offered a reward for information about their activities and has made a lot of positive noises about pursuing those responsible – but, in reality, there has been very little real action.

Direct censorship is not the problem in Colombia. "It is not something that is made public, it is not the shutdown of sta-

tions, of the media," says FLIP. Instead, "it is stigmatisation, the threats which arrive by mail, to your house, your work". And the government's tendency to stigmatise certain subjects contributes to the culture of self-censorship. FLIP's executive director Andrés Morales claims that "many journalists believe that if they don't write about sensitive issues, they won't be punished for their words".

This is a reality regional reporters in Colombia recognise only too well. A recent survey of 700 journalists by press monitoring group the Antonio Nariño Project found 79 per cent of them admitting that they engaged in self-censorship.

Nydia Serrano of El Universal, who has seen some of her colleagues flee the country after receiving death threats, concurs: "The

In 2012, there were 158 direct attacks on journalists

number of journalists killed is down, as is the threat … and we feel more secure. The statistics are correct, but that's because we don't tell about 80 per cent of what happens in this country."

The situation is exacerbated by the scale of impunity from conviction. FLIP claims 87 per cent of the 140 killings of journalists in Colombia since 1977 have gone unpunished.

In 2012, two investigations – into the murders of Jon Félix Tirado and José Domingo Cortés – had to be dropped after they exceeded the statue of limitations. Ten investigations expired in 2011. Since 1977, 59 of the cases have been dropped after state prosecutors simply ran out of time. The statute of limitations on five further unsolved murders will expire by the end of 2014. In 2011 authorities only punished three out of the 23 attacks on journalists by state employees. For many, this is evidence that authorities lack the will to adequately protect journalists and prosecute those who →

→ commit crimes against them. In some cases, when asked, authorities refuse to provide information about who is in charge of particular cases.

And, in order to fight self-censorship, FLIP is increasingly helping journalists publish their work away from their home turf. When journalists don't publish for security reasons, says Andrés Morales, "we help to create agreements or alliances with national media or other outlets so the work can be published".

But such actions are a drop in the ocean. Colombia's deteriorating media environment has prompted renewed calls for action. As Karen Granero, Latin America director for the International Federation of Journalists, points out, "the culture of impunity for crime against journalists must end. Press freedom can never thrive in the absence of the rule of law. Whilst many people talk about restitution for the victims of the conflict, the peace talks are creating new victims." And, she adds, those journalists "tackling impunity" and helping to create a safer environment in which they can pursue their work without fear of threats is "a vital part of the peace process".

In the run-up to the 2014 presidential elections and the end-of-year deadline for a final agreement at ongoing peace talks, human rights campaigners fear the situation will get worse.

According to the International Media Support organisation, paramilitary groups and criminal gangs opposed to both current peace talks and land reform proposals are stepping up attacks against the press. Colombia will remain in the spotlight, one of the most dangerous countries in the world to practise journalism.

"Committing acts of violence against journalists is not a new phenomenon, but that doesn't mean the recent events are not alarming," said Fabio Posada, head of the investigative unit of El País, one of Bogota's leading newspapers. "The high degree of impunity sends a message to society, especially to criminals: that journalists are not important. You can kill them and nothing happens." ☒

©Jeremy Dear
www.indexoncensorship.org

Jeremy Dear is a freelance journalist living and working in Ecuador and Colombia

13) WOMEX
THE WORLD MUSIC EXPO

LATERATE
★ 27 SEP ★
2013
DEADLINE

Networking

Showcase Festival

Trade Fair

Conference

Film Screenings

Awards

virtualWOMEX

Cardiff, Wales, UK

23–27 Oct 2013

www.womex.com

American dreams

42(3): 106/108 | DOI: 10.1177/0306422013503067

Will surveillance revelations impact the reputation of the United States as a global democratic leader? **Matthew Shears** reports

"COME BACK WITH a warrant" is a pre-Revolutionary War principle that helped shaped the identity of the United States. The Fourth Amendment is at the heart of Americans' sense of self, but as the disclosures about government surveillance continue, they are being forced to grapple with potential limits to this seemingly fundamental right. And the US as a whole is starting to see its reputation as a global leader and democratic force challenged.

For many Americans, openness in government and transparency are also fundamental pillars of a democratic society. This is the world view espoused by the US, and other Western nations, in the growth and development of the internet. Edward Snowden's revelations clearly will not only hurt the US's reputation but also its credibility in promoting an internet characterised by democratic freedoms.

The US has promoted an internet driven by entrepreneurs, consumers, and businesses, and underpinned by a community of technical organisations running day-to-day operations, with only minor roles for governments or international organisations. However, this is a view that is increasingly challenged by a group of nations that see a much greater role for the state in economic and political matters related to the internet. Some of these nations do not share the same outward commitment to internet freedom and are well known for their surveillance-based,

human-rights-infringing regimes. Snowden's revelations appear to unmask many Western nations as wielding similar surveillance programmes. The internet freedom world view expressed by the US, and supported by other Western governments, is in danger of ringing hollow.

In the fractured world of global internet policy, the consequences of these surveillance activities will become quickly apparent. As cybersecurity concerns increasingly come to the fore in policy discussions, the Snowden disclosures are likely to reinforce the view among many nations that more stringent state controls over the internet, under the guise of national security, are necessary – arguing that they are "just doing what the US is doing". The US and other governments have been keen to keep internet issues out of the ambit of international organisations and government-to-government decision-making structures. But the pervasive and extra-territorial nature of surveillance programmes will only reinforce those calling for centralised, government-driven policy initiatives in institutions that operate on a one-country-one-vote system. Finally, those nations in the midst of building regulatory and institutional frameworks to support an internet economy may now be convinced that the imperative of security should take precedence over openness, transparency, and other principles that underpin the internet's success. →

QUIET
RESPECT
PLEASE

→ At the moment these challenges are going unaddressed. The US is engrossed in a national debate over the degree to which its NSA programmes have infringed the rights of Americans. In Europe there are criticisms of the US's activities, but there is more than a whiff of hypocrisy in the air. The political establishment in the United Kingdom has circled the wagons around its pervasive surveillance activities. At some point, though, these nations are going to have to recognise that security cannot come at the price of privacy and that surveillance does not trump all. They will need to demonstrate a real commitment to human rights for all citizens, in their respective territories and beyond. Otherwise, emphatic speeches about the importance of internet freedom will amount to just talk. ☒

©Matthew Shears
www.indexoncensorship.org

Matthew Shears is director of the project on global internet policy and human rights at the Center for Democracy and Technology, based in Washington, DC

LEFT: In the Gettysburg address, President Lincoln spoke of the struggles ahead for the US in its establishment of new freedoms

Risky business

42(3): 109/112 | DOI: 10.1177/0306422013502910

A raft of new gag laws in the United States are making it harder for investigative journalists to expose food industry scandals, **Andrew Wasley** reports

THE CALL CAME early in the end. Around seven. We were on, our contact said. Tonight was the night. We'd been waiting most of the day after last night's plans had been aborted at the eleventh hour. Staff at the hotel's reception must have thought it odd that three guests were heading out at nearly midnight. This wasn't a place with nightlife.

The taxi picked us up, as arranged. The driver had been paid well above the going rate for this and wasn't interested in the details. Privately, he must have thought it was unusual. Ferrying two foreigners and a fellow countryman deep into the Polish countryside, dropping them off in the middle of nowhere, returning at a predetermined time unless – as we'd warned him – he got a call stating otherwise.

As the car lights disappeared slowly into the night, someone approached. The security man. He spoke with our translator in haste before beckoning us through the unlocked gate. Across a piece of rough ground, towards one of several vast shed-like buildings set in a row. You could smell it was a farm well before it looked like one. The unmistakable waft of animal waste and straw and feed and chemicals.

Inside, with the door now closed behind us, hundreds of young pigs were visible under the dazzling artificial lights. We didn't have long. The security man had returned to his post outside, to smoke cigarettes and re-read the same paper he'd been reading all evening. He would be watching his clock closely.

The pigs were crammed in; moving, squealing, eating, shitting – these animals didn't have the luxury of outdoor exercise or daylight. This barn (more like a warehouse in fact) was home for now. Locals told us the farm contained 13,000 pigs, and was an intensive piglet "nursery", where young animals were brought from breeding establishments elsewhere to fatten up before being dispatched to the slaughterhouse and people's dinner plates.

We flicked the cameras on – video and stills, as is normal for assignments like this – and recorded what we saw. There were healthy animals, but plenty were lame and injured. One pig had an abnormal growth the size of a grapefruit. Some pigs looked emaciated, others appeared sick, some looked frail. There were dead pigs left abandoned on the ground, live animals rustling around the carcasses.

On the wall, charts recorded the number of animals that had died on specific days, and summarised medical treatment records – the names of antibiotics and other chemicals administered to specific pigs, along with details of the dose.

Time to go, the security man had summoned us. Out through the door, across the rough ground, the taxi was waiting. Handshakes with the security guard – and an acknowledgement of what he'd →

→ enabled. It was tricky and risky, sure, he responded, but what did he care, he was leaving in a matter of days. Good luck with the footage, hope it's useful when it's shown god knows where.

As well as the visual evidence of animal welfare conditions, and proof of the drugs in use (difficult to prove usually), we'd collected testimonies from an ex-employee who had spilled the beans on procedures and processes, and from local people, many of whom were complaining about the pollution and other impacts of having a foreign-owned factory farm arrive on your doorstep unannounced.

Seven US states currently have gag laws...and seven are believed to have laws pending

The locals had taken us to a giant open-air waste lagoon linked to another farm run by the same company. We'd filmed dead pigs floating in the cesspit, along with intravenous needles, plastic gloves and other filth.

Things would have been different if this investigation had been carried out on US soil. That's because colleagues and I could have faced prosecutions. In an attempt to thwart the capacity of undercover activists and investigative reporters reporting on food scoops, recent years have seen a wave of so-called "ag-gag" legislation introduced in many US states.

Seven states currently have "ag-gags" in place, including Iowa, Missouri and North Dakota; seven are believed to have laws pending, including Pennsylvania; and three, California among them, have withdrawn similar legislation. Although details vary from state to state, the premise is the same: to criminalise those who seek to record evidence of animal cruelty (and other abuses) at factory farms or other farm-related locations.

In Iowa, successfully obtaining employment at agricultural premises under false pretences was made illegal in March 2012. In North Dakota, similar legislation was passed as far back as 1991, making it an offence to trespass or create a recording at a farm. In Missouri, a law passed in July 2012 forces an undercover investigator or journalist to officially report any animal rights abuses seen within 24 hours of their discovery.

New Mexico and California have both recently seen "ag-gags" introduced, but the proposed laws were withdrawn following public concerns. In Pennsylvania, legislation currently being considered seeks to outlaw trespass and filming at factory farms.

Such investigations – especially when accompanied by powerful video images – are bad for PR, and thus bad for business. They hit companies where it hurts by shocking consumers and galvanising opinion.

A groundbreaking investigation released in 2008 by pressure group Humane Society of the United States resulted in the largest meat recall in US history, after an undercover worker at the Westland/Hallmark slaughterhouse in California secretly filmed horrific treatment of cattle. The facility had supplied beef to schools across the US.

And campaigners say there is a direct correlation between such image-denting investigations and the roll out of "ag-gags": hot on the heels of "watershed moment" undercover filming by the Mercy For Animals group at Butterball turkey farms in North Carolina, legislation which hampers this kind of journalism was rolled out.

The investigation, the results of which were published in 2011, led to multiple arrests and convictions of workers who were caught on camera maliciously abusing animals, including the first ever felony conviction related to cruelty to farmed poultry in US history. The probe also led to the conviction of a senior Department of Agriculture official for obstruction of justice after she attempted to forewarn Butterball that law enforcement planned to raid the company's facility.

Some commentators believe the current crop of "ag-gags" have borrowed from the model adopted by the controversial American Legislative Exchange Council (ALEC). The powerful lobby group – made up of corporations and politicians – suggests pre-packaged laws, according to its critics, which serve members' vested interests before handing them over, ready to roll, to legislators on a state-by-state basis.

Unsurprisingly, many food corporations and agricultural organisations support ALEC, which in 2003 introduced the contentious Animal and Ecological Terrorism Act, a federal law designed to target radical environmental and animal rights groups.

Some fear that "ag-gags", designed to suppress investigations into factory farming, could be used to target activists and journalists probing other aspects of the food industry.

Recent years have seen an explosion of investigative reporting being used to highlight, amongst other things, exploitation of migrant workers harvesting fruit and vegetable crops, and poor conditions for those toiling unseen in many restaurant kitchens.

The fallout from these investigations can be just as damaging – and costly – as exposés of farm animal cruelty, particularly when the findings provoke a public outcry. In the groundbreaking book Tomatoland, an examination of the tomato growing industry, journalist Barry Estabrook highlighted the shocking case of the "Immokalee babies" born with severe deformities after their mothers were exposed to pesticides whilst harvesting tomatoes.

And, alarming as they are, "ag-gags" are just one of the obstacles and dangers facing those investigating food issues – both in the US and beyond.

Working undercover carries its own inherent risks – not least being caught red-handed whilst wearing a hidden camera or disturbed

ABOVE: Big Boys Gone Bananas! (2011) tells the story of how Dole Food Company sued filmmaker Fredrik Gertten – and successfully lobbied to prevent his documentary Bananas! being shown competitively at the 2009 Los Angeles Film Festival

after entering a property clandestinely – and both activists and journalists, including colleagues of mine, have been threatened or attacked while carrying out their work.

In Brazil, in 2006, one undercover researcher investigating the impacts of the export-led cattle industry was outed in a chilling advert placed in a local newspaper and had to quickly flee the region. His life was judged to be under threat.

In Japan, two investigators were almost killed in 2003 while trying to document the controversial Taiji dolphin hunt. Morgan Whorwood and Brooke McDonald managed to obtain graphic film of the slaughter of striped dolphins, killed for their meat; desperate to seize the footage, fishermen →

→ attempted to throw the pair off a cliff into the sea.

Although they managed to smuggle the footage out – subsequently beamed around the world and temporarily halting the Taiji killing – the activists were forced to leave Japan after receiving death threats.

Legal threats are also a constant peril. Again in Japan, activists from Greenpeace went undercover to expose an embezzlement ring involving crew members working on the whaling ship Nisshin Maru. Following revelations that some of the ship's crew were linked to the illegal sale of whale meat, in 2008, Japanese police raided Greenpeace offices in Tokyo, and the homes of Greenpeace staff; two campaigners – Junichi Sato and Toru Suzuki – were arrested and held in jail for their part in exposing the corrup-

One undercover researcher in Brazil had to flee when his life was threatened

tion. One member of the investigative team cannot return to Japan for fear of being prosecuted.

Those investigating large food corporations also run the risk of being sued for libel. Swedish journalist Fredrik Gertten was targeted by US fruit company Dole Food in 2009 after releasing a documentary, Bananas!, examining the risks to plantation workers' health from pesticides used on company farms. Dole launched a lawsuit against the Gertten documentary and lobbied the Los Angeles Film Festival to have that documentary removed from its bill, leading to allegations of censorship. It was screened, but not as part of the main festival competition.

Similarly, UK filmmaker Tracy Worcester's Pig Business documentary was the subject of several legal threats by pork giant Smithfield Foods in 2008 and 2009. The company sent

four letters to Channel 4 threatening legal action, the last of which was sent an hour before the film was broadcast. As a result of the letter, Channel 4 delayed broadcast of the film and footage was removed in order to make one of the perpetrators less identifiable. The lawyers acting on behalf of the company also contacted London's Barbican arts centre, claiming the film was defamatory and asking them not to show it. The screening only went ahead after Worcester agreed to indemnify the Barbican.

Sometimes, the threats – and the dangers – can be more subtle. While I was investigating slave labour linked to southern Italy's orange and tomato harvests, where thousands of (largely African) migrants suffer brutal exploitation and squalid living conditions, we asked who was really running the show – not the gangmasters, farmers or processors who undoubtedly turn a blind eye to the suffering, but someone else; someone who was benefitting, financially or otherwise, from the racket.

We never had a firm answer. Nobody knew for sure – or would say. It was a question better not to answer. This is mafia country after all. X

©Andrew Wasley
www.indexoncensorship.org

Andrew Wasley is a UK-based investigative journalist specialising in food and the environment. He is a co-founder of the ethical investigative agency Ecostorm, a co-director of the Ecologist Film Unit and was editor of The Ecologist magazine from 2010 to 2012

Rich Mix is a proudly independent three-screen cinema, multi-arts venue and charitable foundation at the heart of East London.

Live Music
Comedy
Spoken Word
Theatre
Family Events
Documentary &
Independent Film

Every penny of our profit is reinvested in creative learning and community activities and supporting emerging artists.

Last year, we provided local artists with free rehearsal space worth £200,000. Of our 400 cultural events, roughly one third were completely free to attend.

Rich Mix is also home to over 20 creative businesses, employing 300 people.

Become a Rich Mix Member and support our work. For just £30 (individual, £45 joint) you'll get two free cinema tickets and discounted tickets for all films and live cultural events, plus great savings with our partners. For full details see www.richmix.org.uk/membership.

www.richmix.org.uk | 020 7613 7498
35-47 Bethnal Green Road, E1 6LA

Supported by
ARTS COUNCIL
ENGLAND

Done with dictatorship?

42(3): 114/116 | DOI: 10.1177/0306422013502622

To the surprise of many, Yemen seems to be moving smoothly towards its first parliamentary elections for 11 years, but looks can be deceiving. **Iona Craig** reports from Sana'a

IN THE MIDST of Sana'a's illustrious ancient stone and mud-brick tower houses it is easy to believe what the guidebooks tell you: that visiting Yemen is like "stepping back in time to a medieval, long-forgotten past". But that wistful prose can be misleading. Yemen is certainly the forgotten sibling of her regional brethren. Yet the often maligned country of some 25 million people is currently hailed as the nearest thing to a post-2011 revolution success story by the international community and the United Nations.

the sense from many Yemenis is that political elites and old rivals are playing their own game

The UN-sponsored 2011 Gulf Co-operation Council (GCC) transition deal, that brought to an end 33 years of President Ali Abdullah Saleh's rule, set in motion a six-month period of national dialogue, due to reach its conclusion on 17 September. The next step now involves the constitution committee's three-month deliberation before a new constitution is put to a national referendum. Finally, both parliamentary and presidential elections are, somewhat ambitiously, scheduled for next February – the

first parliamentary elections in 11 years – to supposedly conclude the transformation from more than three decades of dictatorship to a new, civil society-based, democratic Yemen.

On paper it sounds relatively straightforward and achievable. However, as with the modern-day "medieval country" description, appearances can be deceptive in this corner of the Arabian peninsula. In reality most guidebooks on Yemen have been gathering dust on the shelves of expectant travellers for at least three years as drive-by shootings, assassinations of military personnel and kidnapping of foreigners have escalated, putting the country on par with only Somalia and Syria in the eyes of the British government's worldwide travel advice for no-go countries.

Saleh's three-decade rule through a power base entrenched in a deeply corrupt system of patronage built on nepotism, personal relationships and divide-and-rule tribal politics has been turned on its head since 2011. In the past 18 months the political elite has fractured, shifted and continues to jostle for fresh positions in the so-called "new Yemen". The all-out war on the streets of the capital in 2011 was curtailed by Saleh's eventual signing of the GCC deal in November of that year. Now, the conflict in the shadowy world of the political and military elites is being played out in a murky and sinister manner via seemingly random attacks, shootings and sporadic bombings, usually erroneously and conveniently blamed on the country's al Qaeda network. A similar pattern of assassinations preceded the civil war between north and south in 1994.

Despite Yemen once again being dragged into the spotlight in August, thanks to its infamous al Qaeda off-shoot, AQAP, and a US-instigated terror plot that unnamed intelligence officials claimed emanated from Yemen, far more significant to the country's future prospects was the re-start of the NDC following the Eid a-Fitr holiday. The southern representatives, led by Mohammed al Ahmed – who returned to Yemen last year after 18 years of self-imposed exile in Britain – set out new conditions for their continued participation in the talks, including transferring any discussions to a "neutral country". These new stipulations may yet cause the NDC to fall at the final hurdle over the critical issue of the southern question.

The future of Yemen's stability lies in the change, or lack of it, brought about by the soon-to-be drafted fresh constitution. Despite the necessity pinned to this perceived catalyst for change, arguably the country's existing document – created when North Yemen and the former southern socialist state of the People's Democratic Republic of Yemen unified in 1990 – was not inadequate. The problem lay in its implementation. Large parts of the existing constitution were ignored under Saleh's reign, as he and his government chose not to adhere to the supposedly legally binding document.

The recent opaque political transposition has left Yemen's new president Abd Rabbu Mansur Hadi – also Saleh's former deputy since 1994 – grappling with military restructuring, in an attempt to at least weaken if not break old embedded allegiances and, through the National Dialogue Conference (NDC), confronting the long-standing issues of southern discontent and calls for secession, as well as the increasingly prolific northern-rebel movement of the Shia-Muslim Houthis calling for autonomy. →

ABOVE: Anti-government protests in Sana'a in 2011

→ The GCC deal and resulting period of national dialogue was Yemen's best and only option to avoid further violence and possible civil war in 2011. But, if the transition period fails to bring the results expected by competing factions, the past 18 months will have been futile.

Similarly, the extent to which the old order of widespread patronage will tolerate being undermined without further violent backlash beyond the current wave of assassinations is unpredictable. In addition, there has yet to be any benefit felt by the wider population, the majority of whom struggle to survive in remote rural areas completely divorced from the politics dominating the main cities.

On the dusty hillside of Yemen's capital, the five-star Movenpick hotel – home to the NDC – dominates the skyline on the eastern edge of the city known locally as Sana'a's green-zone. Close neighbours include the British and US embassies and the former Sheraton hotel, now the fortified residence of American embassy staff where US marines prowl the rooftop. The international community is viewed as not just physically removed from the everyday lives of Yemenis as it looks down on the rest of the capital. Due to foreign diplomats' existence behind high-walled compounds with movements restricted in convoys of speeding armoured vehicles, they are also justifiably seen as being completely detached from the urgent yet basic challenges faced by most Yemenis in their daily quest for food, water and electricity that bears little reflection to the talks being carried out in the Sana'a-centric NDC forum.

While the international community buries itself in the intricacies of helping to build the country's future, the sense from many Yemenis is that political elites and old rivals are playing their own game beyond the conference hall – a game that threatens to drag the country back to past conflicts. As a result critics claim the discussions over the new constitution are superficial, serving only to allow time for competing groups to strengthen their support before either renewed conflict or elections take place which will create new faces overseeing an un-changed system.

To add to the burden of expectation, the issues being discussed and agreed upon during the NDC are not binding. Even as the NDC presents its conclusions to the constitution committee this month there is nothing to stipulate that its findings must be included in the new constitution. And, even if they are, it is still far from certain if this fresh, all-encompassing charter can or will be applied by a new, fledgling system in Yemen, where government control extends to an ever-shrinking fraction of the country. ☒

©Iona Craig
www.indexoncensorship.org

Iona Craig is a freelance journalist based in Yemen. @ionacraig

ON THE GROUND

42(3): 117/118 | DOI: 10.1177/0306422013501765

For many in China, revelations about mass surveillance by the US government highlight the superpower's hypocrisy. But, says media expert **Hu Yong**, they also serve as a reminder of problems at home

Beijing

French newspaper Le Figaro described the tale of Edward Snowden as a mix of spy thriller and farce. And when there is drama, there are heroes and villains: in this case the lone hero faces the mighty America, superpower both online and off – and the villain of the piece.

Even China's official news agency Xinhua put it in such terms in an English-language commentary in June. The Snowden case demonstrated, it said, "that the United States, which has long been trying to play innocent as a victim of cyber attacks, has turned out to be the biggest villain of our age". It continued: "At the moment, Washington is busy with a legal process of extraditing whistle-blower Snowden. Washington should come clean about its record first. It owes, too, an explanation to China and other countries it has allegedly spied on. It has to share with the world the range, extent and intent of its clandestine hacking programmes."

This is some of the harshest language yet to come from China's official media. It was, however, only used in an English language piece, and not officially published for mainland consumption. This might have been because Xi Jinping and Barack Obama recently enjoyed an informal summit, at which China proposed a "new superpower relationship". But more likely it was because the problems Snowden exposed also exist in China – and in China the problem is much worse.

On 21 June, a Caixin.com commentary, What does Prism show?, first explained the debate in the US, then turned to China: "Many Chinese [people] are angry over Snowden's claims the US hacked Chinese networks. But for a rapidly changing China it would be more constructive to ask what this case teaches us about using the rule of law to balance freedom and security. The importance of this goes without saying." The article referred to Wang Lijun, who, as head of the Chongqing Public Security Bureau, far overstepped his legitimate powers to set up a huge and illegal intelligence operation that claimed to be able "to search China's entire identity database in twelve and a half minutes". It went on to say that "this again shows how rampant power can run without independent judicial balances, without supervision by public opinion … how to ensure police and procuratorial authorities do not let another Wang Lijun arise is a major issue for China."

Using the Snowden case to look at China meant that Caixin.com reporters and editors were inevitably labelled "rightist public intellectuals" by China's anti-American leftists. One, posting under the handle of "the shameless Chongqing police", commented on a Xinhua piece that named the US as the "biggest villain" about whom "anyone →

→ in the world with basic judgment skills would reach the same conclusion – except of course China's public intellectuals, who are US lackeys". Media commentators claimed China's liberal public intellectuals had been dealt a heavy blow, with those who usually hold the US up as a model left in crisis. Wang Xinjun, a researcher at the Academy of Military Science, wrote in the People's Daily's overseas 25 June edition that "in a sense, the United States has gone from a 'model of human rights' to 'an eavesdropper on personal privacy', the 'manipulator' of the centralised power over the international internet, and the mad 'invader' of other countries' networks … the world will remember Edward Snowden. It was his fearlessness that tore off Washington's sanctimonious mask."

Snowden already has his fans on China's social networks. Not because he tore off Washington's mask, but because he provides an example: one man, taking on his own government. China's internet users know life under surveillance all too well, and so admire the man who dared expose a government.

Snowden would make excellent if challenging material for a civics lesson on the rule of law, the constitution, of transparency, and of the balance between freedom and security. But in China we are not yet ready for a serious discussion of this case. And so Snowden, for China's internet users, remains a conundrum. ☒

©Hu Yong
www.indexoncensorship.org

Hu Yong is an associate professor at Beijing University's School of Journalism and Communication and founding director of the Communications Association of China (CAC) and China New Media Communication Association (CNMCA). He is the author of Internet: The King Who Rules and The Rising Cacophony: Personal Expression and Public Discussion in the Internet AgeSelf-censorship

Snap shot

42(3): 119/123 | DOI: 10.1177/0306422013502633

As Azerbaijani citizens get ready for next month's elections, it has become increasingly dangerous to report on human rights violations. Art for Democracy's **Rasul Jafarov** and **Rebecca Vincent** look at some of the country's courageous photojournalists, who document what life's really like under President Ilham Aliyev

IN AUTHORITARIAN REGIMES, art can serve as a powerful means of expressing criticism and dissent, subverting traditional means of censorship. Photography is particularly telling, capturing the raw truth and making it difficult for even seasoned propagandists to refute.

These photographs, from Abbas Atilay, Mehman Huseynov, Aziz Karimov, Ahmed Muxtar and Jahangir Yusif, show a side of the capital Baku that contrasts sharply with the sleek, glossy image President Ilham Aliyev's government seeks to portray. They expose a regime determined to silence its critics – journalists, human rights defenders, civic and political activists and even ordinary citizens who take to the streets in protest.

But those who embrace subjects others prefer to avoid, exposing unsavoury truths the Azerbaijani authorities would prefer to keep hidden – such as corruption and human rights abuses – do so at significant personal risk and hardship. As journalists, they face intimidation, harassment, threats, blackmail, attacks and imprisonment in connection with their work, which is seen as direct criticism of the authorities. As artists, they face economic hardship and restrictions on where they can display and disseminate their work.

Most of these images were taken during unsanctioned protests in Baku. Photographers face particular hazards when covering protests in Azerbaijan, as not only can they be injured in the general chaos, but they can also be singled out because of their work. The Institute for Reporters' Freedom and Safety reports that so far in 2013 there have been 17 attacks against journalists and photographers covering protests.

Photographers also face arrest and protracted legal action as a result of their work. Mehman Huseynov faces up to five years in prison on politically motivated hooliganism charges stemming from an altercation with a police officer during protests ahead of the Eurovision Song Contest in May 2012.

The photographers featured in this story are among the few courageous individuals in Azerbaijan who remain willing to take on the risks associated with this work. They need international support and protection →

ABOVE: Narimanov Park, Baku, 15 May 2010. Police forcibly detain a political activist during an unsanctioned protest. Photograph by Abbas Atilay

→   before they, too, become the subjects
rather than the artists. ☒

©Rasul Jafarov and Rebecca Vincent
www.indexoncensorship.org

Rasul Jafarov is the chairman of the Human
Rights Club and project coordinator of the
Art for Democracy Campaign
Rebecca Vincent is Art for Democracy's
advocacy director. She writes regularly on
human rights issues in Azerbaijan

Photo captions

Overleaf, top left: Fountain Square, Baku, 10 March 2013. A political activist during an unsanctioned demonstration protesting the deaths of military conscripts in non-combat situations. Authorities used excessive force to disperse the peaceful protest and detained more than 100 people. Photograph by Jahangir Yusif

Page 119, overleaf, bottom left: Sabir Park, Baku, 11 March 2011. During an unsanctioned political protest in the wake of the Arab Spring, a police officer encourages journalists to take his photo. This was a rare move, which the photographer believes was intended to distract photographers from other aspects of the protest, such as police physically restraining protesters. Photograph by Mehman Huseynov

Overleaf, top right: Shamsi Badalbayli Street, Baku, 2 April 2012. A resident is forcibly evicted from the area where the Winter Garden will be constructed. Approximately 300 complaints have been sent to the European Court of Human Rights related to forced evictions from this area. Photograph by Ahmed Muxtar

Overleaf, bottom right: Fountain Square, Baku, 20 October 2012. Police detain a young opposition activist during an unsanctioned protest calling for parliament to be dissolved after a video was released showing an MP discussing the sale of parliamentary seats. Dozens of activists were detained during that protest. Photograph by Aziz Karimov

See more photos on:
www.indexoncensorship.org/azerbaijan

These photographers will be part of an exhibition in London this winter. For more details, follow @art4 democracy

Shrinking the globe

42(3): 124/125 | DOI: 10.1177/0306422013500181

Until all North Koreans have free speech online, we cannot claim to have a world wide web, says Index blogging competition winner and Warwick University student **Charley-Kai John**

THE WORLD WIDE web is not worldwide. This is the biggest challenge facing freedom of expression in the world.

You see something. You Tweet about it. You post a status on Facebook. You share. You express. While it may not always be obvious at the time, you are flexing your right to freedom of expression. It is an everyday thing that can be found in your pocket or on your desk. Internet access is your tool for commenting on society. I am uploading this to Index right now using the internet.

What little internet access North Koreans do have is used to make their world smaller

It was given to "us" for free. However, the "you" and "us" are subjective. I am speaking about people in Britain, and other countries where web access is widely available. This subjectivity undermines the freedom of expression embodied in the premise of a "world wide" web. Having open internet access is a privilege that many people – including me – often take for granted.

A trending hashtag has the ability to connect people across the world instantaneously, but that does not mean it will be seen by everyone in every country. North Korea is an extreme and yet important example. Technically this is a country where citizens have access to the internet. However, to say it is a country with internet implies full access, not simply access that is limited to certain members of society and heavily censored by the government.

The country recently acquired its own wireless 3G network. But it is a 3G network unlike any other: the two million North Korean citizens who now use this service are unable to access the internet. The official Democratic Republic of Korea twitter account @uriminzokkir cannot even be accessed. A shame for any North Korean wishing to see the same message its government relays daily, regurgitated through a medium designed to expand the world. What little internet access North Koreans do have is used instead to make their world smaller.

A country that is secluded from the internet is secluded from the world. The North Korean government has been able to hold its grasp by limiting access to a world outside the one they have created. An outside world is not a possibility without a world wide web to present it. This access needs to be in the hands and homes of North Koreans because, at the moment, it is an understandably difficult external world to visualise.

On 24 February 2013, journalist Jean H Lee tweeted, "Hello world from comms center in #Pyongyang". It may only be one tweet floating around the twittersphere that day but it is believed to be the first one sent using the country's mobile 3G service. It is also probably one of the last. At one time, those arriving in the country were offered internet access, a privilege denied to North Korean citizens, but even this access has reportedly now been stopped.

I want to see a tweet, not from a journalist, but from a North Korean, expressing views that are not the government's but their own. I want my blog post to be easily accessible in North Korea. The world wide web has turned freedom of expression into a truly global thing, but there is still room for it to grow. ☒

©Charley Kai-John
www.indexoncensorship.org

Charley Kai-John is an English literature student at the University of Warwick

CULTURE

In this section

Step change

42(3): 126/128 | DOI: 10.1177/0306422013502442

As part of a freedom of expression arts workshop in Addis Ababa, Ethiopia, a group of dancers made a metal workshop their stage. Words by **Julia Farrington**. Photos by **Julia Farrington** and **Yacob Bizuneh**

THE PLACE WAS one kind of hell: cramped, overcrowded, men half running through a narrow alley carrying monstrous loads of scrap metal on their backs, the relentless din of hammering on metal, lungs attacked by the corrosive smoke of burning paint and oil. The men who work here making pans and bowls out of defunct oil drums are paid a pittance for each object they produce. Starting as boys, they go on until they are too worn out to work anymore, seamlessly replaced by more younger men. This is the dark heart of Addis Ababa's *mercato*, the largest open air market in Africa. It sells everything – you can even bargain for a new soul there, so they say.

Yacob Bizuneh grew up in and around the *mercato* and knows the men who work there and the short, brutal life cycle of their trade.

He managed to find a route out through his art, studying at Addis's Alle School of Fine Art and Design. Since graduating this summer, he has been one of the participants in Wax and Gold, produced by Netsa Art Village, a project drawing on historic ideas of passing important messages (gold) in a non-threatening and hidden way (covering them with wax). Bizuneh's idea brought contemporary dancers in to perform around the oil-drum beaters to show that something else is possible in this environment, even if only for a few minutes. The steady, overlapping rhythmic hammering provided the ear-splitting sound track and inspiration for their movements, choreographed by Junaid Jemel.

Jemel, who as a child sold tissues on the street to help support his family, started

→ dancing aged ten when he took part in a programme led by British dancer/choreographer Royston Maldoom in 1996, introducing contemporary dance to kids living in the slums of Addis. Junaid, now an international dancer and choreographer, was one of the founding members of Adugna Dance Company, which came out of Maldoom's programme. Central to their work is the commitment to constantly feed these opportunities back into the community.

A project drawing on historic ideas of passing important messages in a non-threatening and hidden way

Not everyone can make a successful career out of the arts, it's not a magic recipe for change, but the young people who started Adugna, and Yacob himself, are inspiring proof of how art can transform lives. Their work to create access to a space and skills to explore, express and exchange ideas provides a dynamic opportunity for people who have been led to believe that their voice, their experience or their story is valueless.

See more photos: www.indexoncensorship.org/ethiopia ☒

©Julia Farrington
www.indexoncensorship.org

Julia Farrington is head of arts at Index

An alternative resistance

42(3): 129/132 | DOI: 10.1177/0306422013500409

Acclaimed Arabic poet **Najwan Darwish** challenges preconceptions about innocence, tradition and the lives of Palestinians

The World Will Be Good

My son, I'm sleeping on the riverbed
and listening to you
as you cross the bridge.
It's for your sake, too,
that I sleep in language:
your words never fail
to wake me.
The world will be good:
there will be nothing but the love
I left you as your inheritance
to weigh down your shoulders,
so share that love,
'split yourself into many bodies'
just like Urwa Bin al-Ward, the son of the rose
(you too have no father but the rose).

*

My son, the cities were jagged
and all of this was so absurd.
Come, let's go to the forest,
jump on my shoulders
and we'll return to our roots,
come and laugh with me,

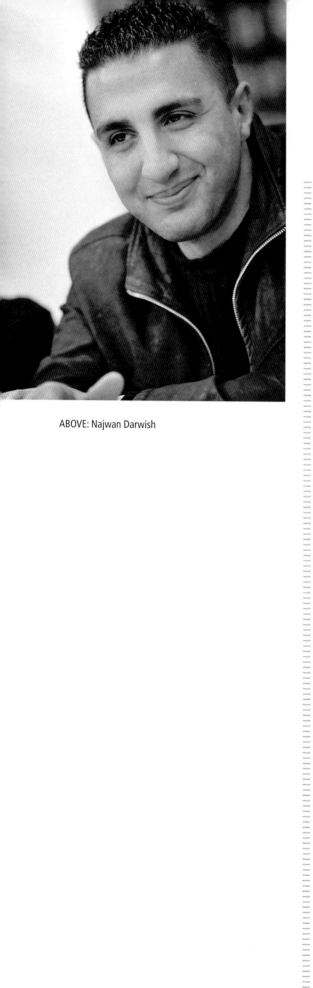

ABOVE: Najwan Darwish

→   we'll cleanse this river with our sound:
in the forest no one will judge us
for our laughter.

*

My son, I missed you on the eve
of Eid al Adha, the great festival.
You would have loved these lanterns
as they swayed to the praises of the Prophet.
I would have woken at dawn
to listen to the hymns.
Is it fear, or is it joy
that makes you tug my hand like this?
Don't worry,
we won't be lost here…
For your sake I woke early
and made my peace
with the festival.

*

From beyond the years,
from beyond the countries and all that the maps conceal,
I guard you
and you guard me.
I'm sleeping on the riverbed and listening
to you as you cross over.

In Paradise

We once woke in Paradise
and the angels surprised us
with their brooms and mops:
'You smell like alcohol and earth;
your pockets are full
of poems and heresies…'
Servants of God, we said, go easy on us.
We long for but a single morning in Haifa:
Our dreams led us here
by mistake.

In Paradise (II)

Even in Paradise
I tossed and turned, writhed in longing;
enchanted by time, I willingly
returned to its bondage,
uncertain of my immortality.
Even in Paradise
all I could think of
was the earth.

The First Hour

A song from Aleppo,
or a poem from Andalusia,
or a ditty from a village
whose people were expelled:
What will visit the sick man
in the New Year's first hour?
This is Haifa, the joy
of God's hands in clay…
Don't say goodbye to her,
it's you who brings her back
now
and forever.
Amen.

An Ass from the Sixties

'I don't ever think during my hours of official duty,
And my life, as everyone knows, has been one long official
duty…'
That's what the employee, who had been awarded the Order of
the Patient Donkey, said to me.
'My wife doesn't think either, nor my children, nor will my
grandchildren think,
Nor do the clouds that pass over our house.
My boy, I'm worried about these thoughts that flit through your
head like grasshoppers.

→ You remind me of myself when I was a young ass back in the sixties:
I used to listen to The Beatles and think about suicide...'
Then he patted me on the shoulder with an affectionate hoof and went on his way,
With blue flies dancing around his stately pair of glasses...

Translated by Kareem James Abu-Zeid ☒

Born in Jerusalem in 1978, Najwan Darwish is one of the foremost Arabic-language poets of his generation. He has gained widespread acclaim for a body of work that both embodies and transcends the Palestinian struggle. Since the publication of his first collection in 2000, Darwish's poetry has been translated into over ten languages. His new collection, Selected Poems, spans over a decade of Darwish's verse and shows the full range of this versatile poet. In it, we see Darwish pushing against both the boundaries of the Arabic language and our preconceived notions of what Palestinian resistance poetry should look like. Resistance, in his verse, takes on many forms, and goes far beyond simply decrying the atrocities of the Israeli Occupation. It seems, in Darwish's verse, that no one is truly innocent, that no one can ever fully escape the tangled webs of politics and lies – least of all the poet himself. It is this tendency towards self-criticism that has, over recent years, turned Darwish into one of the most powerful voices to emerge from Palestine. In 2009, the Hay Festival Beirut39 selected him as one of the 39 best Arab writers under the age of 39.

©Najwan Darwish
www.indexoncensorship.org

No history lessons?

42(3): 133/135 | DOI: 10.1177/0306422013500203

Readers of biographies in Brazil only get to read a rosy version of the truth, as tough legislation grants the subject of the book approval of the draft, or it doesn't make it into bookshops. **Rafael Spuldar** reports on what and why this might change

IN A COUNTRY obsessed by celebrity culture, Brazilian citizens are not allowed to find out stories behind the hype of their favourite local TV stars and musicians or even their least favourite politicians and businesspeople.

Brazil has legislation that only allows authorised biographies on to the bookshelves, and often scandals and other controversial stories around the country's personalities are not exposed.

The country's 2002 reformed civil code made it mandatory for works of a biographical nature – films, books or otherwise – to have prior authorisation from the subject of the work before public release. As a result, most biographies published in Brazil end up being right up the sycophantic scale.

Critics contend that the current legal framework causes editors to practise self-censorship. "Instead of only taking care of the literary quality of the work, editors end up being busy with judicial problems and carrying out a self-censorship that is harmful to the industry", says Sônia Machado Jardim, president of Brazil's National Union of Book Publishers (Sindicato Nacional dos Editores de Livros, or Snel).

Jardim also says that many relatives of people portrayed in biographies try to take advantage of the need for prior approval to demand huge amounts of money, making it expensive to have the books published.

Some cases have become notorious in Brazil. One is the biography of former footballer and two-time World Cup champion Manuel Francisco dos Santos Manuel Francisco dos Santos, generally known as Garrincha, who died in 1983. Written by journalist Ruy Castro, the book was withdrawn from circulation in 1995 because of a lawsuit filed by Garrincha's relatives. The

You can't read or write about Brazil's history any more, you can't produce knowledge. All you have is official stories

author appealed and his work eventually went back on sale.

Singer Roberto Carlos, one of the most popular artists in the past 50 years, not only forced the withdrawal of a biography written by journalist Paulo Cesar de Araújo, but also banned the publication of a Master's degree thesis on Jovem Guarda, the musical movement Carlos was part of in the mid 1960s. In the 1980s, Carlos also obstructed the publication of magazine articles about him. →

ABOVE: Brazil's former President Lula dips into a book

→ "My book was in full flight when it was shot down," author Paulo Cesar de Araújo told Index on Censorship. He says his biography on Roberto Carlos was on

After so many years of fighting to re-establish democracy and freedom of expression in our country, we cannot allow censorship to put its clutches into artistic works ever again

the bestsellers list when it was pulled off the shelves in February 2007, having sold 47,000 copies already, a very healthy figure in a country where there are far fewer frequent book readers than in the USA or Europe.

"You can't read or write about Brazil's history anymore, you can't produce knowledge. All you have is official stories that serve their characters," says Araújo. Snel's Sônia Jardim agrees, arguing that preserving history's knowledge is more important than profit. "After so many years of fighting to re-establish democracy and freedom of expression in our country, we cannot allow censorship to put its clutches into artistic works ever again."

In 2011, controversies like this led deputy Newton Lima (Workers' Party) from São Paulo to draft legislation – nicknamed the Biographies Act – that changes the Civil Code and annuls the need for prior authorization of biographies from public people, like politicians and media celebrities.

"The Civil Code's Article 20 [that makes previous authorisation mandatory for biographic works] makes no sense. The Constitution already gives everyone the right of publicity to protect one's dignity, and if necessary, anyone can go to the courts," deputy Lima told Index on Censorship.

"When people go into public life, it gives everyone the right to protect their dignity, and anyone who feels harmed can go to court," deputy Lima told Index on Censorship. Of course, one does not want to deprive public people of all their privacy, but it certainly gets diminished," says the Biographies Act's rapporteur in Congress, deputy Alessandro Molon (Workers' Party) from Rio de Janeiro.

The Chamber of Deputies' Constitution and Justice Committee passed the draft Bill conclusively in early April, which meant it should have gone straight to a Senate vote. However, deputy Marcos Rogério (PDT Party) from the state of Rondônia filed a petition against it, making it mandatory that the deputies voted before senators – a move that put the Biographies Act on the bottom of the pile of draft Bills.

Rogério justified his petition by saying the draft Bill's language left some issues unaddressed.

"What is public dimension anyway? It's a relative concept. Someone can write, for example, a biography about a city counsellor either accusing him or promoting him electorally. It can be used for good or for evil. The constitution protects both freedom of expression and privacy," the deputy said during a Constitution and Justice Committee debate.

Newton Lima says he has no hope of seeing a vote on his Biographies Act until next year, when a new Congress is to be elected. "If I'm re-elected and nothing new happens until then, I'll do it all over again, I'll present this draft Bill again from the very start."

However, Lima feels optimistic about another move made by a group of publishers called the National Association of Book Publishers (Associação Nacional dos Editores de Livros, or Anel). They filed a direct action of unconstitutionality with the federal Supreme Court in July 2012, arguing that the Civil Code clause governing prior authorization generates censorship, which is prohibited in Brazil.

The federal Attorney-General's office issued a favourable opinion to Anel's action, but Solicitor-General Luis Inácio Adams Roberto Gurgel was opposed to it. Minister Carmem Lúcia is responsible for ruling on the case in the federal Supreme Court. There is no deadline for the court's ruling.

"It's a matter of time for Article 20 to be revoked, because it is so evidently unconstitutional," says Newton Lima. 'It will go down either by an act of the Supreme Court or by new legislation, I'm sure about it."

Author Paulo Cesar de Araújo also feels confident about a Supreme Court ruling that would make the publication of biographies easier – and he already plans to have an updated version of his Roberto Carlos book in the stores. "We still have to know in detail the format this ruling is going to have. But it's certain that my book will be back in one way or another."

However, he points out that opposition is already moving against changes in legislation. Recently Roberto Carlos himself – along with other artists – went to Brazil's capital of Brasília to confer with congress people and even with President Dilma Rousseff to defend Article 20.

This worries Araújo, because he feels the debate about biographies is still not clear to everyone. "I think artists in general don't understand that the present legislation is bad for them. It restricts not only books but film biographies and plays as well, so they have less work."

As writer and politician Winston Churchill famously said: "History will be kind to me, for I intend to write it" – an approach to history that the Brazilian authorities currently seem to support. ☒

©Rafael Spuldar
www.indexoncensorship.org

Rafael Spuldar is a journalist based in Brazil

What's the future for copyright?

42(3): 136/139 | DOI: 10.1177/0306422013501759

Philip Pullman

Copyright is simple to understand, except when those who want to get rid of it start complicating the explanation. If I write a book, the right to make money from it belongs to me, and I make an agreement with a publisher who will print it and distribute it, collect the money it sells for, and pass on a small proportion to me. Anyone who wants to read it either has to buy it, in which case I get that small proportion of the money it sells for, or borrow it from a library, in which case the librarian counts the number of times that title is borrowed, passes on the details to the Public Lending Right administrators, and I'm paid a small sum for each borrowing.

Quite a number of people make money in

> ## It wasn't stealing, he said, it was more like breathing the air that was available to everyone

the course of these processes. The editor, the jacket designer, the publicist, the printer, the library assistant, the bookshop manager, the public lending right administrator, and others, all earn a living on the back of the fact that I and my fellow authors have written books that people want to read. And so do I, and that's as it should be: we all contribute to the process of bringing my book to

the public. Our rewards vary, of course: if my book sells a lot of copies I might make more money in a year than the bookshop manager, whereas if it sells very few I'll make a great deal less. But that's the

Philip Pullman

risk I take, and on the whole this system is fair, and most authors see the justice of it.

What happens when someone buys my book and lends it to a friend? Well, I don't get a penny for that, of course. Nor do I get a penny when they decide they would rather get rid of the book and give it to Oxfam, who sells it second hand. But those transactions are pretty few, and I can put up with the anguish of making no money from them by thinking that, after all, they increase the number of my readers, who might buy my next book themselves.

Now suppose that someone sees there's money to be made from books, and decides to print and distribute my book themselves, without any agreement with me, and keep all the money they get from it. They'd be fairly stupid to do that, because this is where the law of copyright comes in. They're not allowed to do it. It's against the law. That's why it very rarely happens now, although it used to happen a great deal before international copyright agreements came into existence. Charles Dickens, for example, made no money at all from the vast sale of his books in the United States, and he was justly angered about it.

But nowadays that sort of thing doesn't happen. Except … Someone invented the internet. And instead of going to the great difficulty and trouble of printing, binding, distributing, and so forth, in order to steal someone else's literary or musical work, all the thief has to do is press a few keys, and they can make our work available to anyone in the world, and take all the money for themselves. This is most familiar to us in the field of music, of course. The ease and swiftness with which music can be acquired in the form of MP3 downloads is still astonishing even to those of us who have been building up our iTunes list for some time.

Some of us take the moral route, and pay for it, but many don't. I had a long argument with a young man a year or two ago, a bright, decent student who was going to work in the field of the arts himself, who maintained that he had a right to download anything he wanted without paying for it, because it was there and he could do it. What about the money you're stealing from the artist? I asked. Well, first of all it wasn't stealing, he said, it was more like breathing the air that was available to everyone; and secondly, making music was something the musician would do anyway, as a hobby, and downloading it wouldn't stop them from doing it; and thirdly, if they wanted to make money they should do as other musicians did, and perform live gigs, and go on tour, and sell merchandise at the door.

Then there's YouTube. The pianist Krystian Zimerman was recently playing at a festival in Essen, Germany, when he spotted a member of the audience filming him on a phone. He stopped playing and left the stage,

and "explained on his return that he had lost recording contracts in the past because his playing of the works in question had already been uploaded onto the internet where people could see it for free," according to BBC Music Magazine.

Books are slightly different, but the principle is the same. The internet only shows up in stark terms how like a cobweb the law of copyright is when confronted with the sheer force wielded by large corporations.

As Richard Morrison wrote in BBC Music Magazine, Google has been adept at fostering the impression that it is merely an altruistic and democratic "platform" – a digital version of Speaker's Corner – rather than a commercial publisher that is as accountable to the laws of copyright, libel and theft as any old-fashioned "print" publisher would be. That "Google has managed to sustain this illusion of being something like a charity or public service is astonishing, since it is a massively profitable global corporation with ways of minimising its tax bill that many would consider to be the opposite of public-spirited." (At the end of the article, Morrison writes:" 'If you quote me, I promise not to sue.')

The technical brilliance is so dazzling that people can't see the moral squalor of what they're doing. It is outrageous that anyone can steal an artist's work and get away with it. It is theft, as surely as reaching into someone's pocket and taking their wallet is theft. Writers and musicians work in poverty and obscurity for years in order to bring their work to a pitch of skill and imaginative depth that gives delight to their audiences, and as soon as they achieve that, the possibility of making a living from it is taken away from them. There are some who are lucky enough to do well despite the theft and the piracy that goes on all around them; there are many more who are not. The principle is simple, and unaltered by technology, science, or magic: if we want to enjoy the work that someone does, we should pay for it. →

→ **Cathy Casserly**

The world is changing. Being a creator means something different today from what it meant a few years ago. And, let's be honest, the change hasn't been all good. The seemingly endless parade of newspapers shutting their doors or slashing their budgets is a stark reminder that it's hard to make a living as a content creator. Today's writers, photographers, and musicians must think very creatively about how to distribute and monetise their work, and the solutions they arrive at may look very different from the ways previous generations of artists made money.

Copyright closes the door on countless ways that people can share, build upon, and remix each other's work

Recently, there has been a lot of discussion about Spotify and similar music-streaming services and whether they pay artists fairly. The debate underscores the larger issue, that traditional distribution models are quickly becoming obsolete. The new generation of artists must be as cutting-edge with its business models as it is with its art.

According to world-renowned science-fiction author Cory Doctorow, "My problem is not piracy, it's obscurity." Years ago, Cory decided that making it easy for people to download his books would do more for his career than trying to make it hard would. In other words, Cory doesn't see people accessing and sharing his work online as a threat; he sees it as his livelihood. In a lot of ways,

Cory represents the new possibilities for creators in the digital age. The creators who are thriving today are the ones who use internet distribution most innovatively; in fact, the ones who are most generous with their work often reap the most reward.

But copyright was created in an analogue age. By default, copyright closes the door on countless ways that people can share, build upon, and remix each other's work, possibilities that were unimaginable when those laws were established. For Cory and artists like him, people sharing and creatively reusing their work literally translates into new fans and new revenue streams. That's the problem with the all-or-nothing approach to copyright. The All Rights Reserved default doesn't just restrict the kinds of reuse that eat into your sales; it also restricts the kinds of reuse that can help you build a following in the first place.

I work for Creative Commons, a global non-profit organisation that offers a set of open content licences that lets creators take copyright into their own hands. By licensing her works under one of these, a creator can turn All Rights Reserved into Some Rights Reserved, permitting others to reuse her works as long as they properly attribute her and, if she chooses, comply with one or two additional conditions. We're not anti-copyright; in fact, our tools go hand-in-hand with copyright. Without the strength of copyright protection behind them, the conditions of a Creative Commons licence would be unenforceable. Our licences are written by expert copyright lawyers and have been upheld in court numerous times.

What's more exciting than the licences' track record in court is their impact on the world. Writers, musicians, and filmmakers are using our tools to build new creative communities and redefine how artists share, collaborate, and monetise. Scientists and other researchers are publishing their papers and data openly, letting others carry their work forward more swiftly. Governments are starting to require open licensing on resources and research that they fund, ensuring that the public has full access to what it paid for. Educators are building textbooks and other educational resources that anyone can use and customise at no cost, helping to bring higher quality education to communities with limited resources.

Of course, open licensing alone isn't what makes a creator successful. Cory is successful because he's a gifted and hard-working writer. Amanda Palmer is famous thanks to her songwriting talent and charisma. Jonathan Worth wouldn't be a sought-after photographer if he didn't have a knack for taking perfect shots. These people aren't successful because of Creative Commons. But they are successful, in part, because they found ways to let the power of the internet carry their careers to new heights. And for each of them, that strategy included sharing their work widely under an open licence.

It's impossible to imagine how new technologies will redefine the next generation of creative professionals, but I believe that the most innovative creators won't try to go back in time. Instead, they'll use new technologies to their own benefit and that of their peers. They'll carry technology forward rather than trying to fight it back. I can't wait to see what's next. ☒

©Philip Pullman and Cathy Casserly
www.indexoncensorship.org

Philip Pullman is the president of the Society of Authors
@philippullman

Cathy Casserly is chief executive of Creative Commons
@cathycasserly

Index around the world *by* **Mike Harris**

INDEX EDITORIAL

42(3): 140/141 | DOI: 10.1177/0306422013500612

FREEDOM OF EXPRESSION online continues to be one of Index's most important priorities. As whistleblower Edward Snowden's revelations about the US National Security Agency's (NSA) mass surveillance of US and non-US citizens show, digital rights are, and will continue to be, a crucial issue for free speech advocates everywhere. It's clear that some democratic governments engage in covert surveillance with little or no judicial oversight. Under the USA's FISA 702 law, authorities can carry out arbitrary searches and create sophisticated pictures of the lives of huge numbers of individuals.

This doesn't just impact upon privacy but also on the right to freedom of expression: if an individual no longer believes they can communicate online in private, they will self-censor, worry about who they associate with and be careful about what to say. Index continues to prioritise digital freedom at both the global and national level. Index staff participated in key international events and summits in Stockholm, Tunis and also at World Press Freedom Day. In mid-June Index joined Middle East and North African internet activists in Tunis for the Freedom Online Coalition conference. The anger there was palpable, as was a real sense that the US was opening the door for authoritarian states to undertake far wider surveillance than they already do, as well as establishing a norm for surveillance as a matter of routine and not only in clearly defined, exceptional circumstances.

Index calls on governments and politicians to condemn population-wide mass surveillance. We also urge the US to stop its heavy-handed treatment of whistleblowers such as Edward Snowden and Private Bradley Manning, a 2011 Index Freedom of Expression Award winner who spent nine months in solitary confinement. Index is also undertaking advocacy initiatives to shape and impact on EU freedom of expression guidelines, which will help determine how the EU interacts with non-European countries on free speech.

In May, in the same week the NSA revelations were made public, Index published Heading in the Right Direction on Digital Freedom?, a report arguing that many of the EU's digital policies limit digital rights rather than enhance them and calling for the establishment of a coherent strategy for ensuring these rights. With public attention focusing on freedom of expression online, it's time for the EU to act, not only on the issue of mass surveillance — it must also take up its responsibility to protect free expression more widely. Together with its partners from across Europe, Index has launched a pan-European petition to drive public awareness and put pressure on EU leaders to stop mass surveillance.

The International Freedom of Expression Exchange (IFEX) annual conference, held in June in Cambodia, reminded us that the challenges to freedom of expression are as forceful as ever. IFEX partners, including journalists, artists and activists, shared their experiences of the ways in which free speech is censored, outlawed and vilified - as well as their accounts of continued attacks and intimidation.

In July, Index joined artists at a conference in Addis Ababa to discuss artistic freedom of expression. In Ethiopia, free speech has come under attack by a paranoid government that is using vague anti-terror legislation to silence opposition voices. Artists are using their talent and skills to fight back against this repression.

Index also undertook in-depth work on both artistic and wider free speech and media freedom issues in Burma. In March, Index co-hosted a high-profile symposium in Rangoon, assessing the challenges artists face today. It was led by comedian and activist Zarganar, whom Index and others campaigned for when he was handed down a 59-year prison sentence in 2008. Index launched a report on free expression in Burma on 15 July, the same day that the country's president, Thein Sein, visited London. The report, Burma: Freedom of Expression in Transition, reveals that reform to the country's draconian legal framework is making slow progress and calls on the EU and the US to increase pressure on the president to outline how wider change will be implemented.

From the global threat to free expression posed by mass surveillance to specific national and regional issues, Index's work is needed now more than ever. With both democracies and authoritarian regimes curtailing free speech, finding a way to ensure it is not undermined is arguably more difficult than ever before. ⊠

©Mike Harris
www.indexoncensorship.org

Mike Harris is head of advocacy at Index on Censorship

On freedom of expression

42(3): 142/144 | DOI: 10.1177/0306422013500179

Though the free speech environment has shifted dramatically since Index on Censorship began publishing 40 years ago, the challenges are still strikingly familiar. Outgoing Index chairman **Jonathan Dimbleby** charts the changes

SNOWDEN. CYBERSPACE. SECURITY. Wikileaks. Leveson. Libel. Privacy. Pornography. Facebook. Twitter. The buzzwords tumble forth amidst a firestorm of confused debate about rights and wrongs. At the heart

> **A crusading alliance of cruelly ill-used victims, bruised celebrities and lapsed libertarians was ready to give politicians the ultimate and permanent authority to license the press – and thereby on what should and should not be published in a free society**

of the matter is a precious human right, a defining characteristic of a civilised society – the right to free expression.

More than 40 years ago, when Index opened a window against the stifling, foetid world of censorship in the Cold War, its focus was on Eastern Europe, where the voices of the intelligentsia were muffled and their typewriters were obliged to hack out the party line. Then it seemed so clear, so very black and white. I witnessed the Eastern Bloc as a reporter, and I saw the repression and the fear. I had secret rendezvous with brave individuals who could never express a free thought in public without courting arrest, and I pitied their humiliation. When the wall came down in 1989, I walked from West to East through Checkpoint Charlie. A forlorn East German border guard stamped my passport and a while later, authorised by no one, I clambered out again by the Brandenburg Gate, feeling that giddy elation of the moment that promised to be a New World Order in which freedom would rule and all would be well.

At University College London, I had been weaned on John Stuart Mill and Jeremy Bentham. So compellingly did they set the terms of a moral and political debate about rights, responsibilities and freedoms that to this day I set my compass by their convictions. And my experiences as a globetrotting reporter, especially in Africa and Latin

ABOVE: The Berlin Wall, 1989

America, gave me ample and horrifying evidence to confirm my prejudices in favour of those two great thinkers. I met tyrants and dictators and their victims – those few who were brave enough to talk to me with their faces hidden from the camera to protect themselves and their families from imprisonment, torture, or death. It seemed – it was a no-brainer – the denial of free expression for hundreds of millions of people across the planet was, unequivocally, a crime against humanity.

Today it is both the same and very different. The principles have not changed but the context is altered. In this century there are a great many shades of grey along the spectrum between black and white. It used to be said – and some still say it – that the only justification for restricting our freedom to say what we want by every means of communication is to prevent the immediate prospect of physical harm caused when someone shouts "fire" in a crowded theatre. But this is to beg all the important and interesting questions. Go back to the ten words at the top of this article and ask yourself: do I have a simple answer in the name of "freedom of expression" to the conundrums implicit in all of them? If you do, then I would warn you against being simplistic.

Very few countries in the world now openly suppress freedom of expression. Leaving →

→ aside Russia (which is a depressingly complex case) and relics from the Soviet era like Belarus and most of the "stans", the continent of Europe is free of dictatorial regimes. Great swathes of Africa, Asia, and South America have been liberated from tyranny. Most of us now belong to a world where the mobile phone and cyberspace prevail where – with notable exceptions – the rulers have little choice but to heed the voices of the people, most of whom now have the right to vote in more-or-less free elections. To varying degrees this means that the threats to freedom of expression are universally shared and very similar. But they are also more equivocal: shades of grey again.

Inside every one of those ten words at the top of this piece lies a plausible and at least superficially persuasive argument in favour of arresting or suspending freedom of expression. In Britain, for example, we've seen the phone-hacking scandal. Journalists committed serious crimes, offences that disgust all decent people. But there is already a panoply of laws to balance the competing rights of the individual and society: laws against discrimination, laws that protect official secrecy, laws against libel and defamation (mercifully reformed, thanks to the work of Index and others), laws against contempt of court, laws against bribery and corruption, and – via the European Court of Human Rights – laws to protect privacy as well.

No wonder the rest of the "free world" was aghast to discover that a crusading alliance of cruelly ill-used victims, bruised celebrities and lapsed libertarians was ready to give a parliament of duly elected but "here today, gone tomorrow" politicians the ultimate and permanent authority to license the press – and thereby what should and should not be published in a free society. And no wonder authoritarian governments elsewhere looked on with complacent approval, perhaps asking themselves secretly: "If the mother of parliaments can accrue such control, why shouldn't we?

Their licence is ours as well!" So much for freedom of expression.

I am frequently offended by what others say and write – by their scurrilous gossip, careless cruelty, and unbridled bigotry – but I am even more offended by those who think I do not have the right to be offended. For me that nostrum is a useful lodestar. More importantly, these concerns are not just local British issues. They affect all people and all nations in a world where rapidly growing numbers of tweeters and bloggers – the new moguls of the social media – are writing the rules as they go along. How and why should their absolute freedom to write what they want be constrained by law?

One of the many things I have learned during five years as chairman of Index is that simple questions about freedom of expression invariably have complex answers. Take those ten words with which I started this article, and add others if you will. Then ask yourself a simple question in relation to each of them: is there any limit to freedom of expression that might be justified in this context? In our New World Order – which has acquired a form and a technology that most of us could scarcely imagine when the Berlin Wall fell – this is one of the great challenges facing all those who believe that the right to express oneself freely is indeed inalienable. It is also why Index on Censorship, by testing and challenging those who would muffle this right, matters so very much. X

©Jonathan Dimbleby
www.indexoncensorship.org

Jonathan Dimbleby is outgoing chair of Index on Censorship and a broadcaster and journalist

Language lessons *by* **Padraig Reidy**

INDEX EDITORIAL

42(3): 145/146 | DOI: 10.1177/0306422013500188

Orwell was less than impressed with inaccurate use of English. **Padraig Reidy** feels the same. He argues that lazy journalists are failing to understand the author's writing by tediously using "Orwellian" every time a security scandal comes along

THE REVELATION THAT US intelligence services have allegedly been monitoring everyone in the entire world all the time was good news for the estate of George Orwell, who guard the long-dead author's copyright jealously.

Sales of his novel Nineteen Eighty-Four rocketed in the United States in June as Americans sought to find out more about the references to phrases such as "Big Brother" and "Orwellian" that littered discussions of the National Security Agency's PRISM programme.

The Wall Street Journal even went so far as to describe this profoundly bleak novel as "one of the hottest beach reads this summer". And web editors, hankering after a top ten Google ranking for their articles, quickly commissioned articles on the Orwellian theme.

Meanwhile, news website Business Insider published a plot synopsis that managed to run through the events of the book without describing what the book was about at all. The nadir of this frenzy was reached by an Associated Press correspondent, who wrote of his "Orwellian" experience of being stuck airside at the same Moscow airport as whistleblower Edward Snowden for a few hours (for added awfulness, an editor's note on the piece suggested that this deliberate exercise in boredom was "surreal").

Nineteen Eighty-Four (not 1984) has become the one-stop reference for anyone wishing to make a point. CCTV? Orwellian. Smoking ban? Big Brother-style laws. At the height of the British Labour Party's perceived authoritarianism while in government, web libertarians squealed that "Nineteen Eighty-Four was a warning, not a manual".

It was neither. It's a combination of two things: a satire on Stalinism, and an expression of Orwell's feeling that world war was now set to be the normal state of affairs forever more.

There is no system in the world now, with the possible exception of North Korea ... that can genuinely be said to be "Orwellian"

A brief plot summary, just in case you haven't taken the WSJ's advice on this summer's hot read: Nineteen Eighty-Four tells the story of an England ruled by the Party, which professes to follow Ingsoc (English Socialism). Winston Smith, a minor party member, thinks he can question the totalitarian party. He can't, and is destroyed.

While Orwell was certainly not a pacifist, descriptions of the crushing terror of war, →

→ and the fear of war, run through much of his work. In 1944, writing about German V2 rockets in the Tribune, he notes: '[W]hat depresses me about these things is the way they set people off talking about the next war ... But if you ask who will be fighting whom when this universally expected war breaks out, you get no clear answer. It is just war in the abstract.'

It's hard for us to imagine now, but Orwell was writing in a world in which the Universal Declaration of Human Rights was not yet formulated, and where the Soviet Union seemed unstoppable. Orwell had long been sceptical of Soviet socialism, and for his publisher Frederick Warburg Nineteen Eighty-Four represented "a final breach between Orwell and Socialism, not the socialism of equality and human brotherhood which clearly Orwell no longer expects from socialist parties, but the socialism of Marxism and the managerial revolution". Warburg speculated that the book would be worth "a cool million votes to the Conservative party".

This is the context in which Nineteen Eighty-Four was written, and the context that should be remembered by anyone who reads it.

But too often it is imagined there is a "lesson" in Nineteen Eighty-Four as, drearily, it seems there must be a lesson in all books. There is not. The brutality of Stalinism was hardly a surprise to anyone by 1949. The surveillance, the spying, the censorship and manipulation of history were nothing new. Orwell was not so much warning that these things could happen as convinced that they would happen more. He offers no way out, no redemption for his characters. If this book were to have a lesson, Winston would prevail in his fight against the Party; or Winston would die in his struggle but inspire others. We would at least get far more detail on the rise of Ingsoc (the supposed secret book Winston is given, The Theory and Practice of Oligarchical Collectivism, goes some way in explaining how the Party rules, but doesn't really explain why it rules). As it is, we get an appendix on the development of "Newspeak", the Party's successful project to destroy language and, by extension, thought. This addition is designed only to assure us that the Ingsoc system still thrives long after Winston has knocked back his last joyless Victory gin.

There is no system in the world today, with the possible exception of North Korea (which has barely changed since it was founded just after Nineteen Eighty-Four was published), that can genuinely be said to be "Orwellian". That is not to say that authoritarian states do not exist, or that electronic surveillance is not a problem. But to shout "Big Brother" at each moment the state intrudes on private life, or attempts to stifle free speech, is to rob the words, ideas and images created by Orwell of their true meaning – the very thing Orwell's Ingsoc party sets out to do. ☒

©Padraig Reidy
www.indexoncensorship.org

Padraig Reidy is senior writer at Index